THE FOUNDATIONS
OF AESTHETICS

I. A. RICHARDS
SELECTED WORKS
1919–1938

Volume 1   *The Foundations of Aesthetics* (1922)
Volume 2   *The Meaning of Meaning* (1923)
Volume 3   *Principles of Literary Criticism* (1924)
Volume 4   *Practical Criticism* (1929)
Volume 5   *Mencius on the Mind* (1932)
Volume 6   *Coleridge on Imagination* (1934)
Volume 7   *The Philosophy of Rhetoric* (1936)
Volume 8   *Interpretation in Teaching* (1938)
Volume 9   *Collected Shorter Writings 1919-1938*
Volume 10 *I. A. Richards and his Critics*

C.K. OGDEN
I. A. RICHARDS
JAMES WOOD

THE FOUNDATIONS OF AESTHETICS

Edited by John Constable
LECTURER IN ENGLISH
MAGDALENE COLLEGE
CAMBRIDGE

LONDON AND NEW YORK

First published 1922 by George Allen & Unwin Limited

This edition published 2001
by Routledge
2 Park Square, Milton Park, Abingdon, Oxon, OX14 4RN

Simultaneously published in the USA and Canada
by Routledge
711 Third Avenue, New York, NY 10017

Routledge is an imprint of the Taylor & Francis Group

First issued in paperback 2011

© 2001 The Master and Fellows of Magdalene College, Cambridge
Editorial material and selection © 2001 John Constable
Typeset in Granjon by Libellus, Cambridge.

All rights reserved. No part of this book may be reprinted or reproduced or utilised in any form or by any electronic, mechanical, or other means, now known or hereafter invented, including photocopying and recording, or in any information storage or retrieval system, without permission in writing from the publishers.

British Library Cataloguing in Publication Data
A catalogue record for this book is available from the British Library

Library of Congress Cataloging in Publication Data
A catalog record for this book has been requested.

ISBN10: 0-415-21732-6 (hbk)
ISBN10: 0-415-48841-9 (pbk)

ISBN13: 978-0-415-21732-3 (hbk)
ISBN13: 978-0-415-48841-9 (pbk)

ISBN 0-415-21731-8 (set)

CONTENTS

Selected Works of I. A. Richards 1919–1938
Introduction	vii
Acknowledgments	ix
Chronological Checklist of Works	x
I. A. Richards: Life and Works	xxv
Editions and Collections	xlvi

Foundations of Aesthetics
Frontispiece	lvi
Editorial Introduction	lvii
Preface to the Second Edition	1
Original Preface	2
Illustrations	4
The Foundations of Aesthetics	9
1. Aesthetic Experiences	11
The Sense of Beauty	12
2. Beauty as Intrinsic	17
3. Imitation	19
4. The Medium	23
5. Genius	28
6. Truth	30
Mysticism	31
7. Illusion	33
8. Social Effects	35
9. Expressionism	37
Eclecticism	38
Psychological Views	40
10. Pleasure	45
11. Emotion	47
12. Significant Form	50
13. Empathy	55
14. Synaesthesis	62
Education	67
Early Speculations	69
Modern Psychology	72
Index of Names	78
Passages Quoted	79
Editorial Appendix: Preface to the First Edition of 1922	80

INTRODUCTION

This set gathers the major writings of I. A. Richards between 1919 and 1938, including a large proportion of his periodical journalism together with a selection from previously unpublished manuscript articles now held in the Richards Collection of Magdalene College, Cambridge. The aim of this edition has been to provide modernised and corrected standard texts of these classics of twentieth century literary theory, and also to make available for research less accessible books and articles.

The set is arranged chronologically, but the shorter works have been gathered together in one volume, Volume 9, and a further volume, 10, contains a selection of the more important critical articles discussing Richards' works from this period. The volumes are as follows:

1. *The Foundations of Aesthetics*

2. *The Meaning of Meaning*

3. *Principles of Literary Criticism* (With *Science and Poetry*, 1926, as an appendix)

4. *Practical Criticism*

5. *Mencius on the Mind*

6. *Coleridge on Imagination*

7. *The Philosophy of Rhetoric*

8. *Interpretation in Teaching*

9. *Collected Shorter Works 1919–1938*, including the short books *Science and Poetry* (1935), *Basic Rules of Reason*, and *Basic in Teaching*.

10. *I. A. Richards and his Critics*

Each volume, with the exception of Volume 9, has an introduction, and contains a selective checklist of reviews and other discussions relating to the text. Volume 1 contains a general overview of Richards' entire career.

As a general principle I have employed the last authoritative text as the copy text, and consulted all significant editions in the preparation of the text. Textual introductions are provided at the beginning of each volume, or, where required, of individual works within volumes. Aside from the correction of obvious errors considerable liberty has been taken with punctuation, with spelling, and with the layout of the text, particularly with the indentation of quoted matter. It is hoped that the improvement in the appearance of the books, and the ease with which they can be read, will be sufficient justification. To facilitate reference, the page numbers of earlier printings are provided in the margin of the current edition.

Although some degree of uniformity in the style of accidentals has been attempted, certain features, such as footnote reference styles have been left largely as found, though in the interests of clarity certain contractions have been expanded.

ACKNOWLEDGMENTS

I wish to express my gratitude to the Master and Fellows of Magdalene College, Cambridge, for generously permitting me to undertake this edition, giving me free access to the Richards Collection in the Old Library, and supporting me in the later stages of its preparation by allowing me to set up the edition's office in a College room, once I. A. Richards' own, and then in the Old Library itself. Dr Richard Luckett, Fellow of Magdalene and literary executor of the estate of I. A. Richards, has been an unfailing source of advice and assistance.

The preparation of the texts in this edition has involved the co-operation of many colleagues, students, and friends. I would like particularly to thank Ysa Laurel and Matthew Bailey, then undergraduate students at Kyoto University, Japan, who worked with me as editorial assistants in the initial phase of the generation of the computer texts in 1999. Carly Toplis, also an undergraduate student at Kyoto University, carried out additional keyboard work. Stephen Watson, of the Department of Typography, Reading University, assisted me in proofing and emending Volumes One through to Seven, and designed the books, supervising the typesetting, and constructing the specialized fonts required. Stephanie Rehkuh, then an undergraduate in the University of Cambridge, assisted me in proofing and emending Volumes Eight, Nine, and Ten.

For advice and other assistance my thanks to two fellow Ricardians: Yuzuru Katagiri, of Kyoto Seika University, Japan, and John Paul Russo, of the University of Miami. Ian MacKillop, of Sheffield University has answered queries about F. R. Leavis's relationship with I. A. Richards; and John Haffenden, also of Sheffield University, has kindly shared information relating to Richards' friendship with William Empson. Jason Harding, of Feng Chia University, Taiwan, and Jim McCue have both commented on Richards' relationship with T. S. Eliot.

CHRONOLOGICAL CHECKLIST OF THE WRITINGS OF I. A. RICHARDS, 1919–1938

The following chronological checklist provides details of all Richards' known publications in the period 1919–1938, including periodical items later reprinted as parts of books. Only brief descriptions are given of book publication histories; for further details see the various volume introductions. Chapters and sections reprinted in textbook collections have not been recorded here.

For listings of Richards' publications up to his death see J. P. Russo, 'A Bibliography of the Books, Articles, and Reviews of I. A. Richards', in Reuben Brower, et al., eds, *I. A. Richards: Essays in his Honor* (Oxford University Press: New York, 1973), 319–365, and Russo's subsequent listing of additional material in *I. A. Richards: his Life and Work* (Johns Hopkins University Press: Baltimore, 1989), 679–682. Any errors or lacunae of which I am aware in these listings as they refer to the period 1919–1938 have been corrected and supplied below, without, I hope, introducing new errors of my own. Three items incorrectly attributed to Richards have been removed.[1]

Unless otherwise indicated below I. A. Richards is the sole author. In cases of joint authorship the sequence of the authors' names follows that of the original publication. The sequence of items is chronological in order of publication as far as that is known.

---

[1] Adelyne More, 'What is a Fact?', *Cambridge Magazine*, 10/1 (1920), 41–2. Reprinted in *Meaning of Meaning* as Appendix E. Adelyne More, 'Vision and Imagination: A New Basis for Physics', *Cambridge Magazine*, 10/2 (1921), 101–3. Unsigned. 'Thoughts, Words and Things', *Cambridge Magazine*, 11/1 (1921), 29–31. See 'Introduction' to Volume 2 of this edition, *The Meaning of Meaning*, for further details.

1919

1. 'Art and Science – I', *Athenaeum*, No. 4652 (27 June 1919), 534–5. ('Art and Science – II', which followed on 6 June 1919 was by H. W. Crundell.)
2. 'Emotion and Art', *Athenaeum*, No. 4655 (18 July 1919), 630–1.
3. 'Four Fermented Aesthetics', *Art & Letters*, 2/4 NS (Autumn 1919), 186–93.
4. 'The Instruments of Criticism: Expression', *Athenaeum*, No. 4670 (31 Oct. 1919), 1131.

1920

5. 'Preface' to Claude McKay, *Spring in New Hampshire and Other Poems* (Grant Richards: London, 1920).
6. Unsigned, 'The Linguistic Conscience', *Cambridge Magazine*, 10/1 (Summer 1920), 31. Perhaps co-authored with C. K. Ogden. Reprinted in *Meaning of Meaning* as epigraphs and 'Preface'. Although unsigned, this piece should presumably be taken as part of the following item, 'Symbolism', below.
7. C. K. Ogden and I. A. Richards, 'Symbolism', *Cambridge Magazine*, 10/1 (Summer 1920), 32–40. Reprinted in *The Meaning of Meaning* in Chapters 1, 2, 5, 6, and 10.

1921

8. C. K. Ogden, I. A. Richards, James Wood, 'The Sense of Beauty', *Cambridge Magazine*, 10/2 (Jan.–Mar. 1921), 73–93. Reprinted as *Foundations of Aesthetics* (1922), and used in Chapter 7 'The Meaning of Beauty', of *The Meaning of Meaning*.
9. I. A. Richards and C. K. Ogden, 'The Art of Conversation',

Cambridge Magazine, 10/2 (Jan.–Mar. 1921), 94–100. Reprinted in *The Meaning of Meaning* in Chapters 1 and 6.

10. I. A. Richards and C. K. Ogden, 'First Steps in Psychology', *Psyche*, 2/1 (July 1921), 67–79.

11. 'What Happens When We Think', *Cambridge Magazine*, 11/1 (1921), 32–41. Reprinted in *The Meaning of Meaning* (1923) in Chapter 3, with material from pages 35–37 providing material for Appendix B.

12. C. K. Ogden and I. A. Richards, 'The Meaning of Meaning', *Cambridge Magazine*, 11/1 (1921), 49–57. Reprinted in *Meaning of Meaning* as Chapter 9.

13. I. A. Richards, and C. K. Ogden, 'On Talking', *Cambridge Magazine*, 11/1 (1921), 57–65. Reprinted in *The Meaning of Meaning* as Chapter 10.

14. Review, *Mind*, 30/120 NS (Oct. 1921), 483. Review of L. Cazamian, *L'Évolution psychologique et la Littérature en Angleterre (1660–1914)* (Félix Alcan: Paris, 1920).

15. Review, *Mind*, 30/120 NS (Oct. 1921), 491. Review of De Witt H. Parker, *The Principles of Aesthetics* (Silver, Burdett: Boston, 1920).

16. Review, *Mind*, 30/120 NS (Oct. 1921), 491. Review of Charles Lalo, *L'Art et la view sociale* (Librairie Octave Dion: Paris, 1921).

1922

17. *The Foundations of Aesthetics* (George Allen and Unwin: London, 1922). Co-authored with C. K. Ogden and James Wood.

1923

18. Review, *Mind*, 32/125 NS (Jan. 1923), 119–20. Review of

Otto Jespersen, *Language: Its Nature, Development and Origin* (George Allen & Unwin Ltd: London, 1921).

19. 'The Future of Grammar', *Cambridge Magazine*, 11/2 (Early Spring 1923), 51–6. Reprinted in *The Meaning of Meaning* as Appendix A.

20. *The Meaning of Meaning: A Study of the Influence of Language upon Thought and of the Science of Symbolism*. Co-authored with C. K. Ogden. With an introduction by J. P. Postgate, and supplementary essays by Bronislaw Malinowski, 'The Problem of Meaning in Primitive Languages', and F. G. Crookshank, 'The Importance of a Theory of Signs and a Critique of Language in the Study of Medicine'. London and New York, 1923.

21. 'Psychology and the Reading of Poetry', *Psyche*, 4/1 (July 1923), 6–23. Reprinted in *Principles of Literary Criticism* (1924) mostly reprinted as Chapter 16, with other sections appearing in Chapters 13, and 15.

22. D. E. Pilley and I. A. Richards, 'The North-East Arête of the Jungfrau and Other Traverses', *Alpine Journal*, 35/No. 227 (Nov. 1923), 161–5.

1924

23. 'Desire and the Desirable', *Psyche*, 4/3 (Jan. 1924), 213–26. Reprinted in *Principles of Literary Criticism* as Chapters 6, 7, and parts of 8.

24. Review, *Mind*, 33/132 NS (Oct. 1924), 469–70. Review of Herbert Read, ed, T. E. Hulme, *Speculations: Essays on Humanism and the Philosophy of Art* (Kegan Paul, Trench, Trubner: London, 1924).

25. *Principles of Literary Criticism* (Kegan Paul, Trench, Trubner: London, 1925; New York, 1925). Published late November, or December 1924.

1925

26. Review, *Mind*, 34/133 NS (Jan. 1925), 114–15. Review of Henry Rutgers Marshall, *The Beautiful* (Macmillan: London, 1924).

27. Review, *Mind*, 34/135 (July 1925), 383–4. Review of Otto Jespersen, *The Philosophy of Grammar* (Allen & Unwin: London, 1924).

28. 'A Background for Contemporary Poetry', *Criterion*, 3/12 (July 1925), 511–28. Reprinted, with revisions and additions, in *Science and Poetry* (1926) as chapters 5–7.

29. 'Current Literature', *Psyche* 6/1, No. 21, (July 1925), 109–110. Review of Pierre Janet, *Principles of Psychotherapy* , trans. H. M. and E. R. Guthrie (Allen and Unwin: London).

30. 'Science and Poetry', *Psyche*, 6/2, No. 22, (Oct. 1925), 52–66. Reprinted with revisions in *Science and Poetry* (1926) as chapters 1–4.

31. 'Science and Poetry', *Atlantic Monthly*, 136 (Oct. 1925), 481–91. Same essay as preceding entry. Reprinted with revisions in *Science and Poetry* (1926) as chapters 1–4.

1926

32. 'Science and Poetry', *Saturday Review of Literature*, 2 (1926), 833–4. Reprinted with revisions and additions in *Science and Poetry* (1926) as Chapters 5–7.

33. *Science and Poetry* (Kegan Paul, Trench, Trubner: London, 1926), in the Psyche Miniatures General Series. The American edition (W. W. Norton: New York, 1926) was reset and has a different pagination from that of the London edition. The second edition, revised and enlarged (Kegan Paul, Trench, Trubner: London, 1935) does not

appear to have an American edition until it was reprinted in a reset edition with further corrections and additions as *Poetries and Sciences* (W. W. Norton: New York, 1970).

34. With C. K. Ogden, *The Meaning of Psychology* (Harper & Brothers: New York, 1926). Published in the UK as *The ABC of Psychology* (Kegan Paul, Trench, Trubner & Co.: London, 1929. 2nd edition 1930). This volume was published under Ogden's name alone, but there can be no doubt that it is very largely a collaborative work. The case for thinking this book is a joint work is 1. In later life Richards referred to the work as a joint product, in which he was an assistant[1] and did much of the writing;[2] 2. Chapter 10 is based closely on an article published in the *Criterion* over Richards' name; 3. In the preface Ogden acknowledges that he has 'had the advantage of discussing numerous points with my former collaborator, Mr. I. A. Richards […] to whose *Principles of Literary Criticism* I also owe much.'; 4. On. p. 102 of a copy of the First Edition of *Principles of Literary Criticism* (now held in the Richards Collection, Magdalene), there is a holograph marginal note (datable to late 1925 early 1926) which drafts a version of a footnote referring to *Meaning of Psychology*: 'A more detailed discussion from the same angle of the points raised in this and the surrounding chapters will be found in *The Meaning of Psychology* by C. K. Ogden and the author. (Harpers, 1926).' However, in the 2nd edition (July 1926) this reads identically up until the authors' names where it continues 'by C. K. Ogden, where the author's view of mental activity is elaborated'. We may conclude therefore, that in late 1925, early 1926 when the publisher of the book had been found, Richards still

---

[1] See I. A. Richards, 'Co-author of the *The Meaning of Meaning*', in P. Sargant Florence and J. R. L. Anderson, eds, *C. K. Ogden: A Collective Memoir* (Elek Pemberton: London, 1977), 105.

[2] See J. P. Russo, *I. A. Richards: His Life and Work,* 709.

expected his name to be on the book. 5. The diary of D. E. Pilley (later Mrs Richards) records on the 10th of October 1926, that 'Iv. read and discussed parts of his Meaning of Psych.' The reasons for Richards' absence from the title page are unknown.

35. 'Mr. Eliot's Poems', *New Statesman* 26/669 (20 Feb. 1926), 584–5. Reprinted as 'The Poetry of T. S. Eliot' (1926) below, and as Appendix B in the 2nd edition of *Principles of Literary Criticism*.

36. 'Verses and Echoes', *New Statesman* 27/677 (17 Apr. 1926), 16–17. Review of Wilfred Rowland Childe, *Ivory Palaces: Poems* (Kegan, Paul, Trench, Trubner: London, 1925), Teresa Hooley, *Collected Poems* (Cape: London, 1926), C. S. Sherrington, *The Assaying of Brabantius* (Oxford University Press: London, 1925), Barrington Gates, *Poems* (Hogarth: London, 1925).

37. 'The Poetry of T. S. Eliot' in *Living Age* (10 Apr. 1926), 112–15. Reprints 'Mr. Eliot's Poems' (1926) above.

38. 'Books of the Quarter', *Criterion*, 4/2 (Apr. 1926), 372–8. Review of John B. Watson, *Behaviorism* (Kegan Paul, Trench, Trubner: London, 1926). Substantially reprinted as Chapter 10 of C. K. Ogden, *The Meaning of Psychology* (Harper & Brothers: New York, 1926).

39. 'Sentimentality', *Forum*, 76/3 (Sep. 1926), 384–91. Reprinted, revised and expanded, in *Practical Criticism* (1929) as section III.6.

40. 'Count Cagliostro', *Forum*, 76/3 (Sep. 1926), 473–4. Review of W. R. H. Trowbridge, *Cagliostro: The Splendour and Misery of a Master of Magic* (George Allen & Unwin: London, 1926).

41. 'Gerard Hopkins', *Dial*, 81/3 (Sep. 1926), 195–203. Reprinted in a shortened form as 'Gerard Hopkins', *Cambridge Review*.

42. 'Can Education Increase Intelligence: II. But We Can be Taught to Think', *Forum*, 76/ (Oct. 1926), 504–9. Debate with William McDougall.

1927

43. 'The Lure of High Mountaineering', *Atlantic Monthly*, 139/1 (Jan. 1927), 51–7. A shorter version of this piece was published as 'Mountaineering' (1928), below.

44. 'The Changing American Mind', *Harper's*, 154/920 (Jan. 1927), 239–45. Reprinted as 'Are We Becoming More Conscious?' (1927) below.

45. 'Contemporary English Literature: I', *The Osaka Mainichi & The Tokyo Nichi Nichi*, Wednesday, 2 February 1927. Page numbers not known. Clipping in Richards Papers, Magdalene.

46. 'Contemporary English Literature: II', *The Osaka Mainichi & The Tokyo Nichi Nichi*, Thursday, 3 February 1927. Page numbers not known. Clipping in Richards Papers, Magdalene.

47. 'The Meaning of "The Meaning of Meaning"', *The Osaka Mainichi & The Tokyo Nichi Nichi*, Sunday, 6 February 1927. Page numbers not known. Clipping in Richards Papers, Magdalene.

48. 'Are We Becoming More Conscious?', *Psyche*, 8/1, No. 29 (July 1927), 26–34. Reprints 'The Changing American Mind' (1927), above.

49. 'The Teaching of English', *New Statesman*, 29/743 (23 July 1927), 478.

50. 'God of Dostoevsky', *Forum*, 78/1 (July 1927), 88–97.

51. 'Nineteen Hundred and Now', *Atlantic Monthly*, 140/3 (Sep. 1927), 311–17.

52. 'Gerard Manley Hopkins', *Cambridge Review*, 49/1197 (28 Oct. 1927), 49–51. Shortened version of 'Gerard Hopkins', *Dial*, 81/3 (Sep. 1926), 195–203.

53. 'A Passage to Forster', *Forum*, 78/6 (Dec. 1927), 914–20.

1928

54. 'Aspects of the Novel', *Cambridge Review*, 49/1209 (2 Mar. 1928), 304–5. Review of E. M. Forster, *Aspects of the Novel* (Arnold: London, 1927).

55. 'Time and Western Man', *Cambridge Review*, 49/1210 (9 Mar. 1928), 325–6. Review of Wyndham Lewis, *Time and Western Man* (Chatto & Windus: London, 1927). Reprinted as 'Wyndham Lewis' (1929) below

56. 'Mountaineering', *Cambridge Review*, 49/1218 (6 June 1928): 490–492. Reprints in shortened form 'The Lure of High Mountaineering' (1927)

57. 'Books of the Quarter', *Criterion*, 8/31 (Dec. 1928), 315–24. Review of Herbert Read, *English Prose Style* (G. Bell & Sons: London, 1928).

1929

58. 'Cambridge Poetry', *The Granta*, 38/859 (8 Mar. 1929), 359. Review of C. Saltmarshe, J. Davenport, and B. Wright, eds, *Cambridge Poetry 1929* (Hogarth Press: London, 1929).

59. 'Wyndham Lewis', *Tsing Hua Weekly English Supplement*, No. 32 (19 Oct. 1929), np. Reprints 'Time and Western Man' (1928), above.

60. *Practical Criticism* (Kegan Paul, Trench, Trubner: London, 1929).

1930

61. 'Belief', *Symposium*, 1/4 (Oct. 1930), 423–39.

62. Preface for H. E. Palmer, *Interim Report on Vocabulary Selection* (Institute for Research in English Teaching: Tokyo, 1930). Reprinted 1934 or 1935.[1]

1931

63. Interview in the *Harvard Crimson*, February or later 1931.

64. 'Notes on the Practice of Interpretation', *Criterion*, 10/40 (Apr. 1931), 412–20. A reply to Montgomery Belgion, 'What is Criticism?', *Criterion*, 10/38 (1930), 118–39.

65. 'Between Truth and Truth', *Symposium*, 2/2 (Apr. 1931), 226–41. A reply to J. M. M. [John Middleton Murry], 'Beauty is Truth', *Symposium*, 1/4 (Oct. 1930), 466–501.

66. 'Chinese Personal Nomenclature: The Advantages of an Ambilateral System', *Psyche*, 12/1 No. 45 (July 1931), 86–9.

67. Letter to the *Capital Times* (Madison, Wisconsin), 17 July 1931. Copy not seen. Concerns death of S. A. Leonard (see Introduction to Volume 5. *Mencius on the Mind*).

68. 'Criticism of English Poetry', *Yale Review*, 21/1 (Sep. 1931), 191–3. Review of H. W. Garrod, *Poetry and the Criticism of Life* (Clarendon Press: Oxford, 1930), and Charles Williams, *Poetry at Present*.

69. 'The North Ridge of the Dent Blanche', *Alpine Journal*, 43/No. 243 (Nov. 1931), 276–83.

---

1 Source, letter from IAR to David H. Stevens of the Rockefeller Foundation, 2 May 1935 (Rockefeller Archives Center).

1932

70. 'Human Nature: An Early Chinese Argument', *Psyche*, 12/3, No. 47 (Jan. 1932), 62–77. Reprinted in *Mencius on the Mind* (1932).

71. 'Current Literature', *Psyche*, 12/3, No. 47 (Jan. 1932), 93–4. Review of E. S. Bennett, *A Philosophy in Outline* (Kegan Paul: London, 1931).

72. *Mencius on the Mind: Experiments in Multiple Definition* (Kegan Paul, Trench, Trubner & Co.: London; Harcourt, Brace: New York, 1932). Volume 4 of this edition.

73. 'The Chinese Renaissance', *Scrutiny*, 1/2 (Sep. 1932), 102–13. Substantially reprinted in *Basic in Teaching: East and West* (1935).

74. 'Books of the Quarter', *Criterion*, 12/46 (Oct. 1932), 150–55. Review of Max Eastman, *The Literary Mind: Its Place in an Age of Science* (Charles Scribner's Sons: New York and London, 1931).

75. 'Mencius on the Mind', *Times Literary Supplement*, 31/1601 (6 Oct. 1932), 711. Letter to the Editor. Concerns Arthur Waley's *TLS* review of *Mencius on the Mind* ('Mencius on the Mind', 31/1598 (15 Sept. 1932), 634.

76. 'The Problem of China', *Cambridge Review*, 54/1322 (2 Dec. 1932), 149–50. Review of Lionel Curtis, *The Capital Question of China* (Macmillan: London, 1932), and William Hung, ed., *As it Looks to Young China: Chapters by a group of Christian Chinese* (Student Christian Movement Press: London, 1932).

1933

77. *Basic Rules of Reason* (Kegan Paul, Trench, Trubner: London, 1933).

CHRONOLOGICAL CHECKLIST   xxi

78. 'Lawrence as a Poet', *New Verse*, 1 (1933), 15–17. Review of D. H. Lawrence, Last Poems. (Orioli, Florence).

79. 'Preface to a Dictionary', *Psyche*, 13 (1933), 10–24. Sections reprinted in *Basic in Teaching: East and West* (1935). (After Volume 12 *Psyche* became an annual and carried no information concerning month of publication.)

80. 'Meaning and Change of Meaning', *Psyche*, 13 (1933), 185–96. Review of Gustaf Stern, *Meaning and Change of Meaning* (Elanders: Göteborg, 1931). Sections reprinted in *Basic in Teaching: East and West* (1935).

81. Review, *Modern Language Notes*, 48/1 (Jan. 1933), 64–5. Review of Ralph B. Crum, *Scientific Thought in Poetry* (Columbia University Press: New York, 1931). Substantially reprinted in *Basic in Teaching: East and West* (1935), 53–4.

82. Review, *Scrutiny*, 1/4 (Mar. 1933), 406–10. Review of C. K. Ogden, ed, *Bentham's Theory of Fictions* (Kegan Paul, Trench, Trubner: London, 1933).

83. 'Obituary: Professor Piccoli', *Cambridge Review*, 54/1325 (3 Feb. 1933), 209.

84. 'Raffaello Piccoli, Professor of Italian', *Magdalene College Magazine*, 10/3 (1933), 65–7. Shortened revision of *Cambridge Review* obituary.

85. 'Fifteen Lines from Landor', *Criterion*, 12/48 (Apr. 1933), 355–70.

86. 'Our Lost Leaders', *Saturday Review of Literature*, 9/37 (1 Apr. 1933), 509–10. Sections reprinted in *Basic in Teaching: East and West* (1935).

87. 'A Denial', *The Japan Chronicle*, 23 Apr. 1933, 2. Letter to the editor.

1934

88. 'Multiple Definition', *Proceedings of the Aristotelian Society*, Volume 34, Containing the Papers read before the Society during the Fifty-fifth Session, 1933–1934 (Harrison & Sons: London, 1934), 31–50. Also printed in *Basic Rules of Reason* (1933), as Chapters 1–2.

89. 'The Sense of Musical Delight', *Psyche*, 14 (1934), 88–99. Reprinted in *Coleridge on Imagination* (1934) as Chapter 5.

90. 'What is Belief?', *Nation*, 139/3602 (18 July 1934), 71–4. Reprinted in *Poetries*.

91. *Coleridge on Imagination* (Kegan Paul, Trench, Trubner: London, 1934; New York, 1935). Volume 6 of this edition.

1935

92. *Basic in Teaching: East and West* (Kegan Paul, Trench, Trubner: London, 1935).

93. 'Definiteness', *Psyche*, 15 (1935), 77–87. Reprinted in *Interpretation in Teaching* (1938) as Chapter 9.

94. 'The Indian Bridle', in Conrad Kain, *Where the Cloud-Can Go*, Edited, with additional chapters, by J. Monroe Thorington, (American Alpine Club: 1935), 419–26. The First Edition was a 500 copy subscription edition. The first trade edition appeared in 1954 from Charles T. Branford: Boston.

95. 'Books of the Quarter', *Criterion*, 14/55 (Jan. 1935), 308–11. Review of Alice D. Snyder, ed. *S. T. Coleridge's Treatise on Method* (Constable: London, 1934).

1936

96. 'Logical Machinery', *Psyche*, 16 (1936), 76–99. Reprinted in *Interpretation in Teaching* (1938) as Chapters 21–2.

97. 'Empson's Poems', *Cambridge Review*, 57/1399 (14 Feb. 1936), 253.

1937

98. *The Philosophy of Rhetoric* (Oxford University Press: New York and London, 1936). Published January 1937.

99. 'Basic English in the Study of Interpretation', *Psyche*, 17 (1937), 35–47. Reprinted in *Interpretation in Teaching* (1938) as Chapter 11.

1938

100. *Interpretation in Teaching* (Routledge & Kegan Paul: London; Harcourt, Brace: New York, 1938). Volume 8 of this edition.

101. A *First Book of English for Chinese Learners* (Orthological Institute of China: Peking, 1938). Mimeographed manual.

102. C. K. Ogden and I. A. Richards, edited by Adolph Myers, *Times of India Guide to Basic English*, (Times of India Press: Bombay, 1938). Part IV, pp. 55–88, 'Basic versus Word Magic', is by Richards alone.

I. A. RICHARDS: LIFE AND WORKS

Ivor Armstrong Richards was the most influential literary theorist writing in English in the second and third decades of the twentieth century. His impact on the teaching of English literature was immense, both through his own writings (mainly *Principles of Literary Criticism*, 1924, and *Practical Criticism*, 1929) and through his pupils at Cambridge, such as William Empson. Moreover, Richards' discussion of and insistence upon the importance of poetry, by which he often meant literature or, still more generally, 'art', was a controversial but invigorating brief for two generations of writers. Marginalized in literary circles by his work on improvements in language teaching technique, and overshadowed by the post-structuralist movements of the latter half of the century, his importance was for a time obscured, but it is gradually becoming clearer that Richards' attempt to provide a naturalistic account of the values reported by readers of literature is unique in the honesty and thoroughness with which he attempts an integration with the psychological science of his day, and remarkable in the quality of its introspection.[1]

Richards was born in Sandbach, Cheshire, in 1893, the third son of Mary Anne Haigh and William Armstrong Richards, a chemical engineer who managed the district's alkali works. His childhood was happy, marred only by the early death of his father in 1902, and apparently uneventful. While attending Clifton School he contracted pulmonary tuberculosis which enforced a period of rest at a private clinic on Dartmoor, where he read voraciously. In 1911 he went up to Magdalene College,

---

[1] The following short account of his life and works is lightly referenced, and the reader should consult the separate volume introductions for *The Meaning of Meaning* (Vol. 2), *Principles of Literary Criticism* and *Science and Poetry*, 1926 (Vol. 3), *Practical Criticism* (Vol. 4), *Mencius on the Mind* (Vol. 5), *Coleridge on Imagination* (Vol. 6), *The Philosophy of Rhetoric* (Vol. 7), and *Interpretation in Teaching* (Vol. 8), for fuller discussions with extensive citations of documentary evidence to support the history and conclusions here offered in summary form.

Cambridge, to study history. Within a term he had decided that he couldn't continue with this subject, which was simply a record of 'things which ought not to have happened', and changed to Moral Sciences. Although Richards was later to respond to requests to explain the character of this oddly named subject by calling it 'the last word in philosophical savagery', it makes contemporary interdisciplinary courses seem both narrow and shallow. When he eventually took Part One of the Tripos, in 1915, Richards was proficient in contemporary linguistics, philosophy of mind, language, and aesthetics, and was even acquainted with the burgeoning psychological literature, a knowledge he extended in the years following as part of a course of reading designed to support him in the pursuit of a medical career.[1] He considered himself, and was considered by his contemporaries, as a philosopher with psychological interests, and his earliest publications, all in 1919, are philosophical papers in aesthetics ('Art and Science', 'Emotion and Art'; 'Four Fermented Aesthetics'; 'The Instruments of Criticism: Expression').

In 1918 a chance meeting with his contemporary at Magdalene, C. K. Ogden, led to a joint project in philosophical linguistics,[2] which they initially thought of under the title 'Symbolism', but was eventually published as *The Meaning of Meaning* (1923). Before this could make much progress Richards was taken up as a lecturer for the newly-instituted English tripos at Cambridge, again largely through good fortune. Despairing of pursuing a medical career, Richards had gone to see his acquaintance Mansfield Forbes, an historian and Fellow of Clare College, in the spring of 1919 to ask for letters of introduction so that he could plan a career as a climbing guide in the Mountain Hebrides (throughout his life Richards was an ardent

---

[1] Letter to Jacob Bronowski, 11 March 1971, quoted in J. P. Russo, *I. A. Richards: His Life and Work* (Johns Hopkins UP: Baltimore, 1989), 64.

[2] See the 'Introduction' to the edition of *The Meaning of Meaning* in this set for further details.

and accomplished Alpinist). Forbes came of a distinguished Scottish family and knew how to address a laird. The business done, they sat and talked about Wordsworth for some minutes, after which, and quite unexpectedly, Forbes picked up the references, observed that he would be 'throwing these out', and invited Richards to lecture for the English Tripos, a proposal that he accepted immediately.[1] English at Cambridge was in its very beginnings, having only been initiated in 1917, and the first examinations set in 1919. Forbes was a central figure in its foundation, along with E. M. W. Tillyard, and most importantly, H. M. Chadwick, Professor of Anglo-Saxon, to whom Richards' name was passed as a 'recognised' lecturer, meaning that he could collect a fee, 15 shillings, for each student attending three or more lectures of the termly eight. Chadwick told Tillyard that all he knew about Richards was that he 'he's got a First in Moral Science and a red nose',[2] but Forbes' recommendation was sufficient, and Richards was soon delivering courses on 'Theory of Criticism', 'Grammar and the Art of Writing', and 'The Novel'.

In the summer of 1920 Richards returned to Cambridge early from a climbing holiday in the Alps, and on meeting a friend, the painter James Wood (brother of novelist Lucy Boston), they discovered a common interest in a technical analysis of the language of art criticism. This seemed liked a good opportunity for Richards and Ogden to apply the definitional rigour of their 'Symbolism' work, and together the three of them wrote a long article, 'The Sense of Beauty',[3] which was later reprinted as *The Foundations of Aesthetics* (1922). Though a short work, its rigour (sixteen senses of the word 'beauty' are analysed) and its insistence on a psychologistic understanding of the beautiful com-

---

[1] See Hugh Carey, *Mansfield Forbes and his Cambridge* (Cambridge U.P.: Cambridge, 1984), 68–9.

[2] E. M. W. Tillyard, *The Muse Unchained: An Intimate Account of the Revolution in English Studies at Cambridge* (Bowes & Bowes: London, 1958), 76.

[3] C. K. Ogden, I. A. Richards, James Wood, 'The Sense of Beauty', *Cambridge Magazine*, 10/2 (Jan.–Mar. 1921), 73–93.

prise a watershed in British aesthetics. For Richards it was a crucial stage in his development. The lectures he was giving in the Michaelmas term of 1920 on 'Theory of Criticism' were outlining for the first time the psychological theory of value that was to be the mainstay of his writings until the early thirties, but it was in this early work with Wood and Ogden that we find the first draft. 'The Sense of Beauty' was in the final stages of completion as Richards was preparing his lectures for the Lent term, and it provoked him to elaborate his theories further, particularly in relation to the distinction, first outlined in this article, between a harmony of impulses, which might lead to concerted action, and an equilibrium, characteristic of the mind's response to the greatest art, which typically produced no outward action at all. Still more importantly this development stimulated a further sophistication of the dual language hypothesis that Richards was working out with Ogden in his 'Symbolism' papers. Instead of remaining content with a simple division of language into scientific and poetic, Ogden and Richards presented language in terms of a combination of functions, with one pole tending towards pure reference, and the other towards pure evocation, with almost all real cases being mixed.[1]

Much of 1921 and 1922 was taken up with the writing of *The Meaning of Meaning*, and the book appeared in early 1923 as one of the first volumes of the International Library of Philosophy, Psychology, and Scientific Method, which Ogden was editing. The volume was widely reviewed, including discussions by John Dewey, Edward Sapir, and Bertrand Russell (all reprinted here in Volume Ten), and was rapidly adopted as standard reading in universities. Its principal positions, a vigorous destructive criticism of hypostasis and its causal account of meaning, anticipate many of the positions of late twentieth-century linguistics and philosophy. Admittedly dated, it is still important as a founding document in Pragmatics, and no thorough under-

---

[1] For a fuller account of this matter see the Introduction to Volume 2, *The Meaning of Meaning*, and the Introduction to Volume 3, *Principles of Literary Criticism*.

standing of any of Richards' subsequent theoretical writing is possible without reference to it.

A College Lectureship at Magdalene (1922), where he taught English and Moral Sciences, had confirmed Richards in an academic career, and he now turned to establishing himself as a theorist of the arts, working on a new project, also intended for the International Library. The book, which Richards began in 1923 and published in 1924 as *Principles of Literary Criticism*, originally carried the much broader title *The Principles of Criticism*.[1] This corresponds better with its aim, which was to 'put the arts, as the supreme mode of communication, in the forefront of all values'.[2] Immediately, a fault in Richards' naturalistic position became apparent, a fault which continued to trouble him for the rest of his life but was never successfully addressed. While adopting the findings of contemporary psychology, and presenting itself as a branch of scientific inquiry, Richards' analysis confused apology for the values of literature with explanatory accounts of the psychological effects which readers reported as valuable. He expected contemporary science to justify traditional evaluations of the arts, as well as provide detailed causal accounts of the mental processes which led readers to believe that they had undergone something valuable. This apologetic aim compromised his naturalism by ruling off whole classes of explanatory account, namely those which propose that while the arts are indeed seen as valuable by those experiencing them, in fact they are either neutral or harmful. In retrospect we can see that no presumption as to the value of the arts should have been made at the outset of the inquiry, but Richards' own response and sense of benefit were themselves so strong that this would have seemed a perverse refusal to acknowledge the obvious.

The major theme of *The Meaning of Meaning* taken up in

---

1 See the list of 'Other Works by the Same Authors', p. iv of *The Meaning of Meaning* (1923), where the book is optimistically announced as already published in 1923.
2 Letter to D. E. Pilley, 19 November 1923, see John Constable, ed., *Selected Letters of I. A. Richards* (Oxford: Clarendon Press, 1990), 27

Principles is the distinction between 'emotive' and 'referential' meaning, the latter being typical of science, and the former of poetry. While a scientific utterance was aimed at the coherence and validity of its references, an emotive utterance might abandon these aims in order to bring about adjustments to the emotional condition of the listener or reader. This position underlies much of the central theory of *Principles*, where valuable emotive utterances are said to be those that bring an individual's impulses, all those continuing internal reactions to the whole sum of their experience to date, into equilibrium. (Curiously, the earlier interest in an emotively induced harmony of impulses does not figure in *Principles*.) Such effects could be achieved, and indeed usually were, by utterances which when regarded as science were defective. The recent growth of scientific discourse, and the increase in its prestige, had resulted in a decline in the standing of the arts, a decline which was catastrophic since the emotional order they made possible was not yet and perhaps never would be forthcoming from the sciences.

In *Principles* Richards aimed to present a coherent theory of the value of poetry in terms of contemporary psychology, and thus to rehabilitate poetic utterance. A crucial problem, however, was that, in Richards' view, the procedures and habits of science were damaging our ability to read and to write poetry, since we were making requirements of it that could only properly be brought to bear on utterances whose principal purpose was coherent and accurate reference. This theme was further explored in one of Richards' best-known volumes, *Science and Poetry* (1926, rev. 1935), in which he introduced the term 'pseudo-statement' to describe emotive or poetic utterance. Widely misunderstood as meaning 'false-statement', the term was intended to suggest that though resembling statements poetic utterances were not properly judged in terms of truth conditions. However, Richards was aware that the treatment of poetry as if it were science was sometimes a precondition for the occurrence of valuable emotional ordering, and this was usually the result of authorial design. His advice was twofold; firstly that authors would be well-advised, and would write stronger poetry, if they avoided making their work dependent on the varieties of belief properly employed when dealing with science, and, secondly, that readers should avoid applying such standards to poetry. T. S. Eliot, in *The Waste Land* at least, was remarked upon as an author 'effecting a complete severance between his poetry and *all* beliefs' (*Science and Poetry*, 1926, pp. 64–5), a garland for which Eliot, who was already well-known to Richards and was to become a close friend, does not appear to have been grateful.

Although concerned with both writerly and readerly practice, it was only with the latter that Richards now occupied himself, turning to the consideration of a very broad range of errors and misconceptions that prevented effective reading. As early as 1923 he had given students at Magdalene groups of unsigned and undated poems for critical comment, the results being, in his own words, 'Strange, beyond report, thought or belief':

> All the Candidates for my prize with only one exception prefer Mrs Wilcox to Landor, Hopkins, Belloc, De Quincey, and Jeremy Taylor at their very best![1]

At the beginning of the academic year 1925/26, just as he was completing *Science and Poetry*, he extended this experiment in a course of lectures, entitled 'Practical Criticism', delivered in the University. Sheets of poems were handed out one week, the attendants were asked to take the poems away with them and write reports on each of the pieces, to be returned, anonymously, the following week. Richards reviewed and then lectured on the reports, which he soon called 'protocols' (from the German *protokoll*, 'record, observation', a term he appears to have taken from his reading in contemporary laboratory psychology).

In 1926 Richards travelled to the US, and for a while lived in New York, meeting Ogden, who was also working there, and revising both *The Meaning of Meaning* and *Principles of Literary*

---

[1] Letter to D. E. Pilley, 20 November 1923, in *Selected Letters*, 28.

Criticism for second editions. His motivation for this travel was partly personal, since Dorothy Pilley, with whom he had long been in love, was working in Canada. After a period climbing in the Rockies they travelled together on the west coast of the United States, and then took ship across the Pacific, marrying in Honolulu at the end of 1926. They honeymooned in Japan and China, where Richards seems to have conducted 'Practical Criticism' courses in Peking, and on his return to Cambridge he gave the course again in the Michaelmas term of 1927. The material gathered, together with that from the 1925 course, including commentaries now known to be by F. R. Leavis, E. E. Phare (later Elsie Duncan-Jones), and Mansfield Forbes, was used to produce his second, and in the view of some his last, masterpiece, *Practical Criticism: A Study of Literary Judgement* (1929). After presenting the poems and extensive quotations from the protocols, Richards proceeded to a methodical discussion of various component functions in meaning, and an exhaustive analysis of various obstacles to successful reading, amongst the most famous of which are 'irrelevant associations', 'stock responses', 'sentimentality', 'inhibition, 'technical presuppositions', and a misunderstanding of the place of 'doctrine in poetry'. A final section proposed various remedial actions that might be taken to improve the standard of reading.

Inadvertently, Richards had sanctioned a method for criticism. What had been for him an experimental technique, a way of sampling the reading skills of an audience, seemed to support an historically impoverished but linguistically exhaustive concentration on relatively short sections of text, preferably on complete texts which were short, a focus for which the climate in Cambridge was already favourable due to the need to render the new subject more nearly a discipline distinct in method from the study of classical languages. Indeed Tillyard's account of the 'revolution in English studies at Cambridge' makes 'Practical Criticism' the central policy of this revolution, but suggests, not entirely flippantly, that it was a concept with roots in the sixteenth century at Cambridge, and, more convincingly, that it was already in circulation when Richards took it up.¹ Tillyard, however, does not note the difference in motivation. Most of Richards' colleagues were attracted to some form of 'practical criticism' since it gave them a clear examination towards which they could teach. As Tillyard himself observes of the introduction of 'practical criticism' into the Cambridge tripos system, as 'Passages of English Verse and Prose for Critical Comment':

> Here at last we could confront the men with the actual texts and test their ultimate literary insight, making them use their own resources entirely.²

Richards' book rapidly became a classic of literary education, and its terms, if not the substance of its advice, was soon being used world-wide. Sometimes the lineage would be obvious and acknowledged, as it is in the text book *Exercises in Criticism* (1931),³ by one of the students who had attended the original courses, David Shillan. Mostly, though, *Practical Criticism* established a prevailing climate while remaining, rather often perhaps, unconsulted in detail. The consequence is that the critical method it is thought to have introduced and to have made respectable is not one which a careful reader of *Principles* would recognize as being derived from Richards. The investigative character of the 'Practical Criticism' courses was neglected, or simply taken as prescription. The practice of giving unsigned and undated texts had been for Richards merely a means of obtaining responses less cluttered by dishonesty and received opinion, but it was widely taken as advocating a particular way of going about criticism. This does not appear to have been Richards' intention at the time, though his later dogmatic antipathy to any interest in the personality of the poet has con-

---

1 E. M. W. Tillyard, *The Muse Unchained*, 21, 103
2 *Muse Unchained*, 109.
3 *Exercises in Criticism* (London: G. Bell & Sons, 1931).

fused the issue.¹ The Richards of 1929 who had entitled the book '*Practical* Criticism' was aiming to distinguish it from the pure theory of its predecessor, *Principles*, and it was supposed to be 'practical' only in the sense that it attempted to give examples of readers actually engaged in criticism, not that the particular conditions of the experiment were in themselves practical and desirable, or were good practice. In fact, readers who approach it under this misconception are likely to be disappointed.[2]

Now an academic literary star, Richards might have been expected to capitalize on his position, but he seems to have felt that the university discipline of English which he had done so much to establish in Cambridge, and to arm intellectually, was not one he wished to encourage further. As early as 1923 he had been writing to a close friend that 'it was iniquitous, profanation, to use literature for such purposes',[3] and this feeling grew stronger rather than weaker, despite his own growing pre-eminence in the field. The practical consequences of this dissatisfaction were not immediately apparent, and it is widely assumed that Richards' later turn to educational theory, language teaching, and Basic English was a decision with roots in the mid and later thirties, but with Richards' papers now available it is becoming clear that he had begun to steer away from literary discussion before *Practical Criticism* was even published. The courses of 'Practical Criticism' he delivered after 1927 asked not for critical discussion but only paraphrase, a shift indicative of his growing interest in the fundamentals of reading method and the teaching required

---

1 See, for example, his essay 'The Future of Poetry', in *The Screens* (Routledge & Kegan Paul: London, 1960), 105–27, and particularly pages 105–8. The essay is also found in *So Much Nearer: Essays Towards a World English* (Harcourt, Brace & World: New York, 1968), 150–82.

2 See for example, F. R. Leavis, *English Literature in our Time and the University* (Cambridge U.P.: Cambridge, 1969), 16, where he writes that the 'relation between Richards' play with the "protocols" and the intelligent practice of criticism, or practical incitement to it, has always seemed to me so indeterminate (it seems carefully that) and so questionable.'

3 Letter to D. E. Pilley, 19 November 1923, in *Selected Letters*, 26.

to improve it. The establishment of the Faculty of English in the last months of the previous year may have contributed to Richards' distaste for the subject, partly because of the increasing bureaucracy and professionalism, false professionalism he would have felt, that it encouraged amongst both teachers and students. Richards had been educated in a wide-ranging subject, and viewed with suspicion the suggestion that English on its own was a sufficient discipline for the intellect. Originally it had been uncommon for students to take English for both parts of their Tripos examinations, and most moved to English after another subject. F. R. Leavis and Basil Willey, for example, initially read history, and Empson began as a mathematician. Under the new Tripos regulations coming into effect in 1928 students with only English to their names became the norm, and soon these men and women would be entering the Faculty as teachers, and the number of graduate students and research projects was set to increase. Richards was dubious about nearly all of these developments. As early as 1929 he was advising T. S. Eliot, who had asked for information on behalf of a friend, that research in English, even in Cambridge, was not worth the trouble:

> Nobody here specially worth working for. Strongly advise *against* coming here except for a historical, preferably medieval, subject. Anyone specially interested in critical, general, problems can safely be warned off, also anyone with any desire to write for himself. We really are no good to them.[1]

In 1931 he addressed the inaugural meeting of Leavis' English Research Association with a paper entitled 'A Case Against Research in English', and much later in his life Richards spoke openly on the professionalization of literary criticism, remarking that he couldn't see what a student who had been educated in this field and no other was to do with their careers except write books about books. He concluded by observing that he

---

[1] IAR to T. S. Eliot, 4 Feb. 1929, Richards Collection, Magdalene College, Cambridge. Hereafter, RCM.

was, in a rustic conservative phrasing that acknowledged the oddity of his position, 'agin' it on the whole'.[1]

Fortunately, he was spared the difficulties of holding these views in Cambridge in the late twenties at the height of his own influence. In early 1929 an invitation to revisit China and lecture at Tsing Hua University in Peking reached Richards, and made him 'wild with excitement'[2] at the thought of escaping Cambridge routine. In May 1929, in the last term at Cambridge before he departed for China via Moscow and the Trans-Siberian Railway, he began to deliver a course of lectures entitled 'Philosophy of Rhetoric' on which he was to work with great intensity over the next six years. Richards' aims were numerous, but the principal focus was the improvement of the methods by which reading was taught in universities. The 'Practical Criticism' experiment had convinced him that not only was the use of literature as an examination subject mistaken, but that the level of reading proficiency, even amongst those specializing in literature, was so inadequate as to make the exercise almost pointless as an education. The outline of the new course had already been sketched in *Practical Criticism*, where he had noted the absence of any systematic treatise on 'the theory of linguistic interpretation', 'the diagnosis of linguistic situations, systematic ambiguity, and the functions of complex symbols' (p. 335). This he hoped to work towards in his new lectures.

In addition he was much occupied with working out a puzzling new line of thought that had opened up during the writing of *Practical Criticism* in 1928, and this was in fact to take precedence over the 'Philosophy of Rhetoric' for the next four years. The question of the status of emotive or poetic meaning was continuing to interest him, and formed the substance of an

---

1 'An Interview Conducted by B. A. Boucher and J. P. Russo', in J. P. Russo, ed., I. A. Richards, *Complementarities: Uncollected Essays* (Harvard University Press: Cambridge, 1976), [254–269], 266.

2 D. E. Richards diary, 16 February 1929, RCM.

extended dialogue with T. S. Eliot over the question of 'Belief'.[1] In the chapter 'Sense and Feeling', and in the Appendix to *Practical Criticism* Richards found himself moving towards the view that emotive utterance might in some very significant way function to communicate thought. As he was to put it in an important but generally overlooked remark buried in this Appendix, 'thought governed by emotive classifications is still thought'.[2]

The first fruit of this new concern with the status of poetic or emotive language was to come, however, in a study of the Chinese philosopher Mencius. In China during 1929–1930 Richards engaged in a series of seminars with colleagues in Peking, learning some basic Chinese, and devising a system of literal translations to give him sufficient purchase on the samples of Mencius' work to produce a volume, *Mencius on the Mind: Experiments in Multiple Definition* (1932). One focus of the volume was the lack of logical order in sentences, and the degree to which the matter communicated was only implicated in the text. (Again, as so often in Richards, analogues with contemporary developments in pragmatics, particularly in Relevance Theory, are easily found.) The other main subject investigated is the utility of suasive utterance in maintaining moral and political order. Mencius' psychology, Richards noted, was not much concerned with the determinable facts, but only with what sort of views about human psychology would be needed to maintain a moral system which had already been accepted as beneficial. One of the questions raised in *Mencius* is whether some similar use of emotively induced harmonies of impulses, a topic which he had not touched on since his Lent 1921 lectures, might not be needed in the West. Running throughout the book there is the never quite substantiated suggestion that Mencius' poetic utterance might in some important but unclear sense be valuable as referential thought. It was a very daring and striking position, signalling a

---

[1] See Introduction to Vol. 10, *I. A. Richards and his Critics*, for a fuller discussion of this episode.
[2] *Practical Criticism*, 354.

major change of emphasis in his handling of the language of poetry, but the difficulty of the book, and its subject matter, seem to have obscured it from most readers.

No matter how promising this material might have seemed, Richards was prepared to leave all these ideas for development by others, and his intention now was to move back towards 'The Philosophy of Rhetoric', his project for re-invigorating the teaching of reading. As *Mencius* was being prepared for the press in 1931 Richards was taking a deeper interest in a new invention by his onetime collaborator C. K. Ogden – a reduced form of English, 'Basic English' – which was to absorb the larger part of his life. While working on the 'Definition' chapters of *The Meaning of Meaning* Ogden and Richards had noted that most words could be defined with a small subset of the language, and Ogden had gone on to note specifically that the auxiliary verbs in English, 'be', 'do, and 'have', could be combined with a handful of the main verbs, such as 'come', 'get', 'give', 'keep', 'let', 'make', 'put', and 'seem', and some prepositions, to substitute for almost all the major verbs in English. From this insight he had produced a reduced vocabulary, consisting of only 850 words in which it was claimed, with considerable truth, that almost all frequently occurring communicative purposes could be successfully handled. Richards' interest was immediately rekindled, partly because it seemed to be an educational tool which might resolve many of the abuses of English language teaching which he had observed in Japan and China, and partly because it related, with almost uncanny neatness, to the problem of paraphrase in the teaching of English as a literary subject. Conventional parsing and paraphrastic exercises had been earlier ruled out as a possible solution to the crisis he had diagnosed in the mid-twenties (*Practical Criticism*, p. 334), but translation into Basic seemed to offer something new.

Initially, he restricted his activity to occasional journalism proselytising on behalf of Basic English, but before long it had become a major component in the development of the trains of thought begun in the courses on the philosophy of rhetoric. In his next book, *Basic Rules of Reason* (1933), which was composed entirely in Basic, Richards set out to provide a short course in the logic that a writer might benefit from if he were aiming to put his thoughts in order. The overall aims of the book were not modest, since logic was, in the view of Peirce, whom Richards had long found an important source of inspiration, 'the ethics of thinking'. This book sank without trace.

His next book, *Coleridge on Imagination* (1934) is best seen as a pair to *Mencius on the Mind* (1932). In his study of Chinese suasive psychology Richards had been revisiting the theory of emotive meaning to investigate its utility in co-ordinating impulses for action. In *Coleridge* he took as his main subject the equilibria which had formed the basis of his theory of aesthetic response in the early books, and attempted to readjust their relationship to science. Its composition seems, however, to have been almost accidental. Taking up Coleridge in desperation – apparently at his wife's suggestion – in early 1932 as a topic for his obligatory Faculty lectures he found himself, slightly to his own surprise, with enough to say to merit a book, and in the latter part of the year he decided to interrupt his other work. But when he actually came to review his lecture notes it seems that the material did not satisfy him, and he dropped the project in favour of *Basic Rules of Reason*. It was re-ignited, a year later, by Eliot's publication in late 1933 of his *Use of Poetry*. Richards felt that Eliot had mishandled Coleridge, particularly his theory of imagination, and had assigned poetry far too humble a status. In January 1934 he determined to resurrect his Coleridge work to make a counter argument, and in the early months of this year he wrote the major chapters with which the book closes, notably Chapter 7, 'The Wind Harp'. These put poetry in a privileged position, and suggest that while science is a reduced form of our knowledge of the world, justified by its technological power, poetic utterance is the only mode in which man can communicate his fullest response to the world. While much of poetry might be *false* as a science, the sense in which it is *true* is of much more profound value.¹

Coleridge on Imagination was generally well-received as an important stage in the standing and the critical rehabilitation of Coleridge himself. It was also taken, with some reason, as marking a sharp turnaround in Richards' relationship with the sciences. Examination of the whole of Richards' career will, however, show that this is more a change of emphasis than a recantation, and that in any case there are very significant signs of this supposed shift in both *Practical Criticism* and in *Mencius on the Mind*. Other readers who had followed Richards from the beginning found it a sharp disappointment, a confirmation that Richards was, after all, too concerned with the abstract, the scientific. Leavis, in a devastating review which set the tone for received opinion concerning Richards for the rest of the century, wrote that 'his literary interests derive from an interest in theory rather than his theory from his literary interests'.² This was unjust personally, but as a description of his academic practice it was correct, and Richards would have seen nothing in this for which apology was necessary. As a theoretician he dealt with those aspects of literature relevant to his theoretical goals; others he left alone, being under no obligation to give continual evidence of the width of his own reading and response.

Having completed the reinvestigation of 'emotive meaning' Richards was now free to take on his major study of rhetoric. He had been lecturing on the subject for several years, and had a mass of notes and material, but lacked time to bring order to it. In late 1934 the General Education Board of The Rockefeller Foundation asked Richards if he would develop the suggestion made in *Practical Criticism* (p. 335, quoted above) that there should be a disciplined study of the methods of interpretation,

---

1   See the Introduction to Volume 6, *Coleridge on Imagination*, for a fuller account of this position and its relation to his earlier views.

2   F. R. Leavis, 'Dr Richards, Bentham, and Coleridge', *Scrutiny*, 3/4 (Mar. 1935), 400. Reprinted here in Volume 10.

and produce a book-length 'Statement' on how his theories could be applied to the teaching of reading, the whole piece to be delivered by the end of 1935. Richards accepted saying that he would use this as an opportunity to distil his 'Philosophy of Rhetoric' writings, but would collect further data by using his 'Practical Criticism' courses in the Lent and Easter terms of 1935 at Cambridge, which were on prose, and he duly began to gather and analyse protocols. While this phase of the Rockefeller work was in progress he was invited to deliver the Mary Flexner lectures at Bryn Mawr in early 1936, and Richards decided to use these as a vehicle for the more readily grasped summary conclusions of the 'Statement'.

Before sitting down to either Richards published another small volume on Basic English, *Basic in Teaching: East and West* (1935), and in a phase of frantic activity between September and December 1935 he wrote the entire text of the 'Statement', eventually published in 1938 as *Interpretation in Teaching*, and most of the Flexner Lectures, now under the title of his old lecture course, *The Philosophy of Rhetoric* (dated 1936 but actually published in January 1937). This latter book was an immediate success, and remains a classic in the study of metaphor, which Richards argued was fundamental to all utterance, and for which he provided the first analytic terminology, naming the material to be communicated the 'tenor', and the means used to convey it the 'vehicle'. It was not long before this work was to seem primitive, but its seminal quality and its place in intellectual history should not be overlooked, rapid obsolescence, in this case, being a tribute to the interest it had stimulated.[1]

The Rockefeller 'Statement' was distributed and used as the discussion text for three days of seminars in the spring of 1936 with leading North American educators, and with this Richards

---

[1] See for instance the place accorded to it by Paul Ricoeur in his *The Rule of Metaphor: Multi-disciplinary studies of the creation of meaning in language*, translated by Robert Czerny, with Kathleen McLaughlin and John Costello (Routledge & Kegan Paul: London, 1978).

seems to have felt the work's task was accomplished. He was for some time uncertain whether it was suitable for book publication, and he planned extensive revisions and rewritings. Eventually, when the pressure of other work became extreme he contented himself with minimal retouching, and it is hard to avoid the conclusion that had he spent more time in boiling down this comprehensive treatment then the resulting book, which Richards regarded to the end of his life as being his most constructive, and was after all the true 'Philosophy Rhetoric', would be better known. But of all his works it is the hardest to grasp, or to summarize briefly. To a casual glance it seems to be a version of *Practical Criticism* discussing prose extracts rather than verse; but the prose selected was not literary, and Richards was not concerned in this case with the inability to read complex and subtle poetry and to distinguish it from the crude and the sentimental, but with the much less entertaining and rather more fundamental incapacity to successfully interpret basic informational and descriptive utterance. Although it has been mined by conscientious teachers, and has its apologists, it remains the least read of Richards' major works. Most surprisingly, it is not uncommon for those, such as Ricoeur, who discuss Richards' handling of metaphor in *The Philosophy of Rhetoric*, to make no reference to the much fuller handling of this topic in *Interpretation in Teaching*.

With the appearance of *Interpretation in Teaching*, Richards' most creative phase came to a close. Immediately after the Bryn Mawr lectures he returned to China, this time with Rockefeller Foundation support, to investigate the application of Basic English in English Language teaching there, and the next two years were fully taken up by this work. However, his efforts were put under severe strain by the Japanese invasion of China in 1938, and the beginning of the European war put a stop to all further activity, though not before he completed his *First Book of English for Chinese Learners*.[1] Anxious to contribute to the war effort

---

1 *A First Book of English for Chinese Learners* (Orthological Institute of China: Peking, 1938). Mimeographed manual.

Richards was persuaded, by T. S. Eliot amongst others, that he could do more in the United States than in England, and he accepted a position in the Department of Education at Harvard University, where he engaged in further research into the teaching of English as a second language, and to enhancing the abilities of those for whom it was a first language. These projects took him to Disney studios where, with the help of professional cartoonists, the first simplified figures for language instruction manuals were worked up from Richards' designs, and were applied in courses for the US Navy's program to instruct Chinese sailors in the use of American military *matériel*. None of this work was new in concept, and most represented a detailed extrapolation of his interest in paraphrase, or to use his own term 'English-English translation',[1] of which evidence can be found as early as 1929 in revisions made to his Cambridge 'Practical Criticism' lectures. Basic English was now predominant in this work, and continued to be central long after he had developed his own slightly extended version, 'Every Man's English' (first used in his translation, *The Republic of Plato: A Version in Simplified English* (1942)).

His major work was now on texts overseen by his English Language Research Inc., based in Harvard. *Learning the English Language, Book One*, anonymously co-authored with a team of colleagues, most notable amongst which was Christine Gibson, appeared in 1942 (*Learning the English Language: Book Two and Book Three*, was published in 1943, and a *Teacher's Guide*, for the series was published in 1945). These texts, now little known, are founding achievements in the modern method of language instruction. *The Pocket Book of Basic English: A Self-Teaching Way into English*, later retitled *English Through Pictures* (1950), appeared in 1945, and led to a series of similar volumes, of which the first to appear were *French Self-Taught with Pictures* (1950; later *French Through Pictures*, 1953), and *Spanish Self-*

---

[1] *How to Read a Page* (W. W. Norton: New York, 1942; Routledge & Kegan Paul: London, 1943), 125.

Taught with Pictures (later *Spanish Through Pictures*, 1953). All used the same fundamental techniques, graded introduction to grammar through concrete situations depicted in minimally distracting stick figure cartoons.

Richards never ceased to publish on literary subjects, but this area of his work was now limited to occasional papers, and was increasingly journalistic in character (the more substantial pieces are collected in *Speculative Instruments*, 1955), though his *Viking Portable Coleridge* (1950), and its long introduction, remains one of the best selections of Coleridge's work. Somewhat surprisingly, he turned to poetry in the later 1950s, publishing *Goodbye Earth* (1958), *The Screens* (1960), and a verse drama, *Tomorrow Morning, Faustus!* (1962). Later volumes of verse include *Internal Colloquies: The Poems and Plays of I. A. Richards* (1972), and *New and Selected Poems* (1978). The verse, which resists the difficulties of form to achieve the prosaic virtues of clarity and sincerity, has never found a wide circle of admirers. Writing to his biographer, John Paul Russo at the end of his life, Richards admitted that he was resigned to this outcome: 'I do know how *out* of current fashion they are. It doesn't do now to have solvable problems in poems. Only undiscussable enigmas command respect.'[1] Objectively, it is striking that Richards, who had done more than most to stress the enigmatic quality of successful poetry, should have thought that there ever had been or could be much enthusiasm for verse of his type.

In the last decade of his life Richards' sense of the magnitude of the problems confronting the world reached such an intensity that his proposed remedies, found for example in *So Much Nearer: Essays Toward a World English* (1968), and *Design for Escape: World Education Through Modern Media* (1968), seem characterized by a febrile and unbalanced salvationist judgment, which has led to their general neglect. In a review of *Philosophy of Rhetoric*, William Empson had remarked that Richards liked to 'pose

---

1 IAR to J. P. Russo, 29 Aug. 1976, *Selected Letters*, p. 199.

a small definite problem and then bound high into the air', after which 'you only see him leaping round the horizon'.[1] This tendency became more acute in the post-war writing. In *Beyond* (1974), for example, which emerged in part from General Education courses given at Harvard, Richards takes up Homer, the Book of Job, and Dante, as prime documents for a discussion of nothing less than 'the sources of human endeavour'. This failure to ensure a proportionate relationship between his subject matter and his ambitions is all the more distressing when it combines, as it very often does, with an irritatingly avuncular tone. In a lecture this might have been bearable, but in print it fatally obscures diagnoses which are often just, and proposals for remedial courses of action which, though rated somewhat too high by Richards, are practical and suggestive.

After his retirement from Harvard, and from Language Research Inc., Richards returned to Cambridge, England, in 1974. He continued to be active in proselytization for improved techniques in language education (see *Techniques in Language Control*, 1974), and in 1979 visited China to lecture on this subject. Suddenly taken ill he returned to England and died on the 7th of September.

---

[1] William Empson, 'Books of the Quarter', *Criterion*, 17/66 (Oct. 1937), 125.

EDITIONS AND COLLECTIONS

Bibliographies are found in John Paul Russo's 'A Bibliography of the Books, Articles, and Reviews of I. A. Richards', in Reuben Brower, et al., eds, *I. A. Richards: Essays in his Honor* (Oxford University Press: New York, 1973), pp. 321–365, and his subsequent listing of additional material in *I. A. Richards: his Life and Work* (Johns Hopkins U.P.: Baltimore, 1989), 679–682. The listings given for the period 1919–1938 in this volume, above, correct and add to these lists.

There are several selections of Richards writings:

Poetries: Their Media and Ends: A Collection of Essays by I. A. Richards, ed. Trevor Eaton (Mouton: The Hague, 1974), is a collection of essays mostly from the post-war period and focussing on literary papers.

Complementarities: Uncollected Essays (Harvard U.P.: Cambridge Mass, 1976), ed. J. P. Russo, collects essays from 1919 to 1975, and is mostly literary critical in content.

Richards on Rhetoric, ed. A. Berthoff (Oxford U.P.: New York, 1991), selects articles and passages from books, with an emphasis on Richards contributions to the theory of teaching English composition.

A Semantically Sequenced Way of Teaching English: Selected and Uncollected Writings by I. A. Richards, ed. Yuzuru Katagiri and John Constable (Yamaguchi Publishing House: Kyoto, 1993), collects a variety of pieces, including selections from *The Teacher's Guide for Learning the English Language* (1945), and focuses on matters of interest to teachers of English as a second language.

Letters from the period 1911–1979 are gathered in John Constable, ed., *Selected Letters of I. A. Richards* (Oxford: Clarendon Press, 1990).

GENERAL CRITICISM AND ACCOUNTS OF THE WORKS OF I. A. RICHARDS

The following selected checklist concentrates on works dealing with two or more of Richards' books in the years 1919–1938, though later pieces, both articles and book length studies, tend to range still more widely over Richards' career. Unpublished dissertations have not been included. Reviews and other discussions relating to a single work are listed in the prefatory matter to the relevant volume.

Book Length Studies

Brower, Reuben, Helen Vendler, and John Hollander, eds, *I. A. Richards: Essays in His Honor* (Oxford University Press: New York, 1973).

Hotopf, W. H. N., *Language, Thought and Comprehension: A Case Study of the Writings of I. A. Richards* (Indiana University Press: Bloomington, 1965).

James, D. G., *Scepticism and Poetry: An Essay on the Poetic Imagination* (George Allen & Unwin: London, 1937). Sections reprinted in Volume 10.

Karnani, Chetan, *Criticism, Aesthetics and Psychology* (Arnold-Heinemann: New Delhi, 1977).

Karnani, Chetan, *I. A. Richards: A Critical Assessment* (Arnold Publishers: New Delhi, 1989).

McCallum, Pamela, *Literature and Method: Towards a Critique of I. A. Richards, T. S. Eliot, and F. R. Leavis* (Gill & Macmillan; Humanities Press: Dublin; Atlantic Highlands, New Jersey, 1983).

Needham, John, *The Completest Mode: I. A. Richards and the Continuity of English Literary Criticism* (Edinburgh University Press: Edinburgh, 1982).

Russo, John Paul, *I. A. Richards: His Life and Work* (Johns Hopkins U.P.: Baltimore, 1989).

Schiller, Jerome, *I. A. Richards' Theory of Literature* (Yale University Press: New Haven & London, 1969).

Sharma, Rad Padarth, *I. A. Richards' Theory of Language* (S. Chand: New Delhi, 1979).

Shusterman, Ronald, *Critique et poésie selon I. A. Richards: de la confiance positiviste au relativisme naissant* (Presses Universitaires de Bordeaux: New Haven & London, 1988).

Other Discussions

Anon., 'Lecture Bomb-Plot Outrage', *Granta*, 41/919 (30 Oct. 1931), 67–9.

Berthoff, Ann E, 'I. A. Richards and the Audit of Meaning', *New Literary History*, 14/1 (Autumn 1982), 63–79.

Bilsky, Manuel, 'I. A. Richards on Belief', *Philosophy and Phenomenological Research*, 12/1 (Sep. 1951), 105–15.

Bilsky, Manuel, 'I. A. Richards' Theory of Metaphor', *Modern Philology*, 50 (1952), 130–7.

Bilsky, Manuel, 'I. A. Richards' Theory of Value', *Philosophy and Phenomenological Research*, 14/4 (June 1954), 536–45.

Blackmur, R. P., 'A Critic's Job of Work', *The Double Agent: Essays in Elucidation and Craft* (Arrow Editions: New York, 1935), [269–302], 287–92. Also reprinted in *Language as Gesture* (New York, 1952).

Brooks, Cleanth, *The Well Wrought Urn: Studies in the Structure of Poetry* (Harcourt Brace and Company: New York, 1947).

Brooks, Cleanth, 'I. A. Richards and the Concept of Tension', in Brower, Reuben, Helen Vendler, and John Hollander, eds, *I. A. Richards: Essays in His Honor* (Oxford University Press: New York, 1973), 135–56.

Butler, Christopher, 'I. A. Richards and the Fortunes of Critical Theory', *Essays in Criticism*, 30/3 (July 1980), 191–204.

Constable, John, 'I. A. Richards, T. S. Eliot, and the Poetry of Belief', *Essays in Criticism*, 40/3 (July 1990), 222–43.

Crane, R. S., 'I. A. Richards on the Art of Interpretation', In R. S. Crane, ed., *Critics and Criticism: Ancient and Modern* (University of Chicago Press: Chicago, 1952), 27-44. Reprinted from *Ethics*, 59 (Jan. 1949), 112–26. Reprinted in Volume 10.

Eastman, Max, 'I. A. Richards' Psychology of Poetry', *The Literary Mind: Its Place in an Age of Science* (Charles Scribner's Sons: New York & London, 1931), 297–317, 339–43. Reprinted in Volume 10.

Eliot, T. S., 'The Modern Mind', in *The Use of Poetry and the Use of Criticism: Studies in the Relation of Criticism to Poetry in England* (Faber: London, 1933), 121–42. Reprinted in Volume 10.

Fekete, John, *The Critical Twilight: Explorations in the ideology of Anglo-American literary theory from Eliot to McLuhan* (Routledge & Kegan Paul: London, 1977).

Fletcher, Angus, 'I. A. Richards and the Art of Critical Balance', in Brower, Reuben, Helen Vendler, and John Hollander, eds, *I. A. Richards: Essays in His Honor* (Oxford University Press: New York, 1973), 85–99.

Foster, Richard, 'The Romanticism of I. A. Richards' *ELH*, 26/1 (Mar. 1959), 91–101.

Gilbert, Katherine, 'The Intent and Tone of Mr I. A. Richards', *Journal of Aesthetics and Art Criticism*, 3/11–12 (1944), 29–48.

Glicksberg, Charles I., 'I. A. Richards and the Science of Criticism', *Sewanee Review*, 46/4 (Oct.-Dec. 1938), 520–33.

Harap, Louis, 'What is Poetic Truth?', *The Journal of Philosophy*, 30/18 (31 Aug. 1933), [477–88] 484–8.

Harding, D. W., 'Evaluations (1): I. A. Richards', *Scrutiny*, 1/4 (Mar. 1933), 327–38. Reprinted in F. R. Leavis, ed., *Determinations: Critical Essays* (1934), 218–43. Reprinted in Volume 10.

Hartmann, Geoffrey H., 'The Dream of Communication', in Brower, Reuben, Helen Vendler, and John Hollander, eds, *I. A. Richards: Essays in His Honor* (Oxford University Press: New York, 1973), 157–77.

Heath, Stephen, 'I. A. Richards, F. R. Leavis, and Cambridge English', in Richard Mason, ed., *Cambridge Minds* (Cambridge University Press: Cambridge, 1994), 20–33.

Hochmuth, Marie, 'I. A. Richards and the "New Rhetoric"', *Quarterly Journal of Speech*, 44/1 (Feb. 1958), 1–16.

Hyman, Stanley Edgar, *The Armed Vision: A Study in the Methods of Modern Literary Criticism* (Alfred A. Knopf: New York, 1948), 303–46.

Isherwood, Christopher, *Lions and Shadows: An Education in the Twenties* (Hogarth Press: London, 1938), 121–2.

Krieger, Murray, *The New Apologists for Poetry* (University of Minnesota Press: Minneapolis, 1956), 57–63, 113–39. See particularly Chapter 3 'I. A. Richards: Neurological and Poetic Organization', Chapter 7 'I. A. Richards: Some Tools for an Organic Criticism', and Chapter 8 'The Transformation of Richards: A Contextual Theory of the Aesthetic Object'.

Leavis, F. R., 'This Age in Literary Criticism', *Bookman*, 83/493 (Oct. 1932), 8–9.

Levin, Harry, *Why literary criticism is not an exact science* (Harvard University Press: Cambridge, Mass, 1967). Pamphlet of lecture delivered in Cambridge, England, at Wolfson Hall on 12 May 1967.

Lewis, Wyndham, 'T. S. Eliot: The Pseudo-Believer', in *Men Without Art* (Cassell: London, 1934), 65–100. Sections reprinted in Volume 10.

Lucas, F. L., 'English Literature', in Harold Wright, ed., *University Studies: Cambridge 1933* (Ivor Nicholson & Watson: London, 1933), [259-294] 260–75.

M., J. M. [John Middleton Murry], 'Beauty is Truth', *Symposium*, 1/4 (Oct. 1930), 466–501.

McLuhan, H. M., 'Poetic vs. Rhetorical Exegesis: The Case for Leavis against Richards and Empson', *Sewannee Review*, 52 (Spring 1944), 266–76.

Nagarajan, S., 'Statements in Poetry', *JSL* (Monsoon 1976), 84-96. Journal of the School of Languages, Jawaharlal Nehru University.

O'Connell, Daniel, 'Poetry and the Natural Standpoint', *Journal of Aesthetics and Art Criticism*, 32/3 (Spring 1974), 323–9.

Pollock, Thomas Clark, 'A Critique of I. A. Richards' Theory of Language and Literature', in M. Kendig, ed., *A Theory of Meaning Analyzed* (Institute of General Semantics: Chicago, 1942), 1–25. Monograph III in the General Semantics Monographs.

Pollock, Thomas Clark, *The Nature of Literature: Its Relation to Science, Language, and Human Experience*: (Princeton University Press: Princeton, 1942), 145–60.

Rackin, Phyllis, 'Hulme, Richards, and the Development of Contextualist Poetic Theory', *Journal of Aesthetics and Art Criticism*, 25/4 (Summer 1967), 413–25.

Ransom, John Crowe, 'A Psychologist Looks at Poetry', *The World's Body* (Scribner's: London & New York, 1938), 143–65. Extensively revised version of an article first published as 'The Psychologist Looks at Poetry', *Virginia Quarterly Review*, 11 (Oct. 1935), 575–92. Reprinted in Volume 10.

Ransom, John Crowe, 'I. A. Richards, the psychological critic, and William Empson, his pupil' in *The New Criticism* (New Directions: Norfolk, Conn., 1941), 101–31.

Righter, William, *Logic and Criticism* (Routledge and Kegan Paul: London, 1963).

Rudolph, G. A., 'The Aesthetic Field of I. A. Richards', *Journal of Aesthetics and Art Criticism*, 14/3 (Mar. 1956), 348–58.

Russo, J. P. 'Introduction' to I. A. Richards, ed. J. P. Russo, *Complementarities: Uncollected Essays* (Harvard U.P.: Cambridge Mass, 1976), vii-xxiv.

Spaulding, John Gordon, 'Elementalism: The Effect of an Implicit Postulate of Identity on I. A. Richards' Theory of Poetic Value', in M. Kendig, ed., *A Theory of Meaning Analyzed* (Institute of General Semantics: Chicago, 1942), 26–35. Monograph III in the General Semantics Monographs.

Tate, Allen, 'Three Types of Poetry', *Reactionary Essays* (Scribner's: New York and London, 1936), 104–10. Reprinted in part in Volume 10.

Thompson, Denys, 'Teacher's Debt', in Brower, Reuben, Helen Vendler, and John Hollander, eds, *I. A. Richards: Essays in His Honor* (Oxford University Press: New York, 1973), 295–302.

Vines, Sherard, *Movements in Modern English Poetry and Prose* (The Ohkayama Publishing Company; Oxford University Press: Tokyo; Oxford, 1927), 190–7.

Vivas, Eliseo, 'Four Notes on I. A. Richards' Aesthetic Theory', *Philosophical Review*, 44/4 (July 1935), 354–67. Reprinted in Volume 10.

West, Alick, 'Dr Richards', *Crisis and Criticism* (Lawrence and Wishart: London, 1937), 61–82. Reprinted in Volume 10.

West, Geoffrey, *Deucalion, or the future of literary criticism* (London; New York: Kegan Paul, Trench, Trubner & Co.; E. P. Dutton & Co, 1930), 72–92. Reprinted in Volume 10.

Wheelwright, Philip, *The Burning Fountain: A Study in the Language of Symbolism* (University of Indiana Press: Bloomington, 1954).

Wheelright, Philip E., 'Poetry and Logic', *Symposium*, 1/4 (Oct. 1930), 440–57.

Wimsatt, W. K., *The Verbal Icon* (University of Kentucky Press: Lexington, 1954).

Wimsatt, William K., and Brooks, Cleanth, *Literary Criticism: A Short History* (Alfred A. Knopf; Routledge & Kegan Paul: New York; London, 1957).

Wimsatt, W. K., 'I. A. R.: What to Say about a Poem', in Brower, Reuben, Helen Vendler, and John Hollander, eds, *I. A. Richards: Essays in His Honor* (Oxford University Press: New York, 1973), 101–17.

THE FOUNDATIONS OF AESTHETICS

EDITORIAL INTRODUCTION

The composition of *The Foundations of Aesthetics* began in late July or August 1920 when Richards, returning unexpectedly early from a summer's mountaineering in the Alps,[1] met James Wood in Cambridge. Wood, already a close friend, began, in Richards' words 'talking art talk to me', and Richards replied by suggesting that they should work with Ogden as a triumvirate and 'Sort out this art talk':

> We did it all in a very queer way. Here is the picture of the three of us doing it. James Wood in the corner bicycling slowly upside down, doing his Muller's exercises, and supplying the ideas. It would be very late at night. Ogden lying on an immense high day-bed he had. We always called it Sardanapalus's Death Bed. Ogden would be on the Death Bed, pen in hand, writing it all down. And I would be walking up and down, doing a good deal of phrasing and rephrasing. The triumvirate would have sessions far into the night, kept going by an ozone machine Ogden had picked up which produced sparks about a foot long and a tremendous smell of the Underground.[2]

Wood's role is not clear, but it seems that the Chinese material which looms so large was his contribution:

> But it was James (Jas) Wood who first awakened my interest in the multiple potentialities of Chinese phrases. We compared different translations of them in a kind of rapture. It was he who brought the Chung Yung into our *Foundations*. Typically, he made 'The Lodge of Leisures' a catchword among us. H. A. Giles had translated the Chinese collection of yarns as *Stories from a Chinese Studio*. Jas Wood pointed out that in the English translation of Soulié de Morant's version it was *Tales from the Lodge of Leisures*. We delighted in having such a name for wherever we might be doing our hardest work. It must have been an

---

1 IAR to D. E. Pilley, 11 July 1920, RCM.
2 'Beginnings and Transitions: I. A. Richards Interviewed by Reuben Brower', in Reuben Brower, et al., eds, *I. A. Richards: Essays in his Honor* (Oxford University Press: New York, 1973), [17-41], 24.

inverse impulse that made us give a really clamant title to the little book we had so enjoyed writing.[1]

The first appearance of the material was in an article, 'The Sense of Beauty', in C. K. Ogden's *Cambridge Magazine*, 10/2 (Jan.–Mar. 1921), 73–93. This piece in fact constitutes the entire text, with many variants, of the book as eventually published, but lacks the illustrations. The volume publication, which appeared in the first weeks of January 1922[2] carried the new title *The Foundations of Aesthetics*. As Richards notes above this is comically portentous for such a small book, and is perhaps as Ogden's friend Philip Sargant Florence has said 'another of C.K.'s characteristically covert jokes'.[3]

The material from the article was also used for Chapter Seven, 'The Meaning of Beauty', in *The Meaning of Meaning* (1923), but the summary there gives no hint of the broader importance of the book for Richards. It has two areas of significance for his thought. Firstly, it provides a concrete testing ground of the definition routines that Ogden and Richards were working out in their linguistic philosophy. Secondly, the impact that the article and the discussions leading to it had on Richards' theory of value, then being worked out in lectures in October–December 1920 and January–March 1921 was very substantial, and this in turn had consequences for the theory of emotive meaning as we see it in *The Meaning of Meaning*.[4]

---

[1] 'Beginnings and Transitions', 31.
[2] See IAR to D. E. Pilley, 16 Jan. 1922, '*Foundations of Aesthetics* are out and *very impressive*, though I say it', in *Selected Letters*, 26.
[3] P. Sargant Florence, 'Cambridge 1909–1919 and its Aftermarth', in P. Sargant Florence and J. R. L. Anderson, eds, *C. K. Ogden: A Collective Memoir* (Elek Pemberton: London, 1977), 47.
[4] See Introductions Volume 3, *Principles of Literary Criticism* and to Volume 2, *The Meaning of Meaning*, for extended accounts of both these points.

REVIEWS
OF *THE FOUNDATIONS OF AESTHETICS*

Anonymous, 'New Books and Reprints', *Times Literary Supplement* 21/1043 (12 Jan. 1922), 30.

Anonymous, 'Briefer Mention', *Dial* 80/2 (1926), 164.

Anonymous, 'Recent Literature: General', *London Quarterly Review* 137 (Apr. 1922), 275.

Anonymous, 'Reviews', *Magdalene College Magazine*, No. 39, 6/2 (Mar. 1922), 58–9.

Empson, William, 'Chronicles: A Doctrine of Aesthetics', *Hudson Review*, 2/1 (Spring 1949), 94–7.

Hungerland, Isobel, 'Reviews', *Journal of Aesthetics and Art Criticism*, 7/2 (Dec. 1948), 171.

Rutter, Frank, [Untitled], *Bookman*, 62/367 (Apr. 1922), 49.

Valentine, C. W., 'New Books', *Mind*, 32/125 (Jan. 1923), 120–1.

NOTE ON THE TEXT

The Foundations of Aesthetics was first published by George Allen & Unwin in 1922, probably in the first weeks of January.[1] It was revised, largely by Ogden (a copy marked by Ogden survives in the Richards Collection) in 1925, this second edition being published by George Allen & Unwin in England, and by International Publishers in New York from imported sheets, with a new title page. The text reprinted here is that of the revised second edition, of 1925, and has been derived from a copy of the American edition. This second edition text is very nearly identical to that of the first edition, but has a new Preface, and a revised version of what is, somewhat misleadingly, called the 'Original Preface'. These revisions to the original preface are few and appear to be motivated only by requirements of space (the second edition avoids repaginating the main text by fitting both new and original prefaces into the same number of pages). However, it appears appropriate, for the sake of consistency, to retain this revised preface, and print the original as an Editorial Appendix.

Minor errors have been corrected, and some contractions expanded. In order to reduce confusion between the numbering of the chapters, the plates, and the Senses of Beauty (in the first and second editions all are numbered with Roman numerals) the chapters are here numbered in Arabic numerals, the plates with letters, and the Senses of Beauty with capitalized Roman numerals.

To facilitate the tracing of references the page numbers of the second edition (which match exactly, with very few exceptions, those of the first edition) have been supplied in the margin of the pages. All internal cross-references, including those of the index, are to these original page numbers. It should be noted that this may occasionally result in two sets of original numbers

---

[1] See IAR to D. E. Pilley, 16 Jan. 1922, RCM, *Selected Letters*, 26.

on the same page of the current edition, since footnotes in the original edition are occasionally allowed to run over on to a succeeding page.

PREFACE TO THE SECOND EDITION

The reprinting of these pages allows us an opportunity of indicating any alterations of view which might seem desirable. But the reception accorded to the book, even in the short time which has elapsed since the first impression appeared, has strengthened our conviction of its serviceableness; and were we writing today neither the general position, nor the particular mode of exposition would be changed. The advantages of a brief laconic argument are appreciated by those who prefer active rather than passive participation.

Some of the problems here treated are more fully dealt with in other works by the same authors. On the Verbal Problem, *The Meaning of Meaning*,[1] on the Theory of Value, *The Principles of Literary Criticism*,[1] and on general Psychological Principles, *The A. B. C. of Psychology*,[2] may be consulted, while additional comment on the technique of the Artist will be found in *Colour Harmony*.[1]

---

[1] London, Kegan Paul; New York, Harcourt, Brace.
[2] New York, Harpers; London, Cambridge Magazine.

ORIGINAL PREFACE

Interest in questions of Aesthetics has been greatly stimulated during the past few years both by a wider knowledge of non-European – particularly of Eastern and primitive – Art, and by the rapid development of Psychology as a science. Traditional methods of approach equally with vague philosophical speculations have been found inadequate, and the need for a new orientation is evident to most students of recent theoretical publications.

In the following pages an attempt is made to present in a condensed form the greater part of accredited opinion on the subject, and to relate the views thus presented to the main positions from which the theory of art-criticism may proceed. It is hoped that in this way it will serve either as an introduction to those who from a literary point of view or as practical artists are interested in the problems which divergences of aesthetic judgements raise, or as a text-book for students of the Theory of Criticism itself. The discussion therefore follows a rather unusual course, its aim being not to bring theories into opposition with one another, but by distinguishing them to allow to each its separate sphere of validity. If verbal conflicts are avoided, there will be seen to be many possible theories of Beauty, not one only, the understanding of which may help in the appreciation of Art.

The attitude of tolerance which this treatment implies may require a corresponding effort on the part of the reader. Much that on first inspection appears inconclusive or obscure, will, it is hoped, be better understood, as the partial separation of the fields dealt with by the different theories is more clearly realized. The theory of Synaesthesis with which our discussion ends is, however, in a special position. As an explanation of the aesthetic experiences described by many of the greatest and most sensitive artists and critics of the past, it may perhaps be regarded as the theory of Beauty *par excellence*.

The appreciation of Beauty, whether in Painting, Music or

ORIGINAL PREFACE

Poetry or in everyday experience, cannot but be developed by a clearer knowledge of what it is and where it may be looked for, and an acquaintance with the opinions of artists and philosophers on this subject will assist those who wish to increase their powers of discrimination and thereby to lay the foundations of a genuine and at the same time personal taste. It should also be noted that by uniting varied qualifications the authors have been enabled to treat the subject in a more catholic fashion than is usual, and to make it less likely that any important aspect of interest to the general reader has been overlooked.

It remains to add a brief reference to the quotations and the reproductions. When no other object is expressly stated, quotations provide a concrete illustration of some critical point discussed in the passage immediately preceding, and are therefore not to be regarded as additional commentary. They are intended mainly as a constant reminder of what the discussion is about, and are given as fully as space permits in order that the reader may have this opportunity of escaping from the scientific language of the argument. And as regards the reproductions, most of which have been specially made for the purpose,[1] it is hardly necessary to add that they are not put forward as the 'Best pictures', nor are they typical in all cases of their period or place of origin. Each, however, adequately illustrates one *or more* of the theories discussed, and it will be obvious that all of them are works of high rank.

---

[1] For permission to photograph the Hogarth (Plate H) we have to thank the Directors of the Foundling Hospital. Plates B, C, and O are the copyright of the Folkwang Verlag, Hagen, i.W., Plate D of Messrs Braun & Co., and Plate G of the International Portrait Service. The Chinese painting on silk (Plate N) is darkened with age and this has made its adequate reproduction a matter of considerable difficulty. In the Frontispiece and Plates F, I, and N, details only are given, as the presentation of the entire picture on so small a scale would have rendered appreciation impossible. We are indebted to Mr C. H. Hsu for writing the Chinese characters which signify the Doctrine of Equilibrium and Harmony.

ILLUSTRATIONS

Frontispiece: Upper Portion of a Cast of a Primitive Greek Statue from the Acropolis, Athens (6th Cent. B.C.) (See Page 75) *British Museum* — 11

		Page
A	Photograph from nature of breaking wave (East African Coast). See page 75.	6
B	Negro Masks. *Folkwang Museum, Hage, i.W.*	15
C	Wooden Image, Africa. *Lübeck Ethnographical Museum*	
D	Lady with an Ermine, by Boltraffio (Milanese, 1467-1516). *Czartoryski Museum, Cracow*	16
E	Colossal Limestone Statue of a Queen of Rameses II (restored) XIX Dynasty. Height 4ft 7 in. *British Museum*	21
F	Princes of the House of Timur in a pavilion. Portion containing a group of ancestors (Indian Mogul School. Early 17th Century) *British Museum*	27
G	Portrait Bust, by Jacob Epstein. *In the sculptor's possession*	29
H	The March to Finchley (Central Portion) by Hogarth (1697–1764) *Foundling Hospital*	34
I	Sepia Drawing 'Don Quixote', by Goya (1746-1828) *British Museum*	43
J	Amaravati Tope. Figures from the great rail (2 cent. A.D.) *British Museum*	44
K	Sepia Drawing, 'A Victim of the Inquisition' by Goya (1746–1828) *British Museum*	49
L	Amaravati Tope. Disc from the great rail, with worshippers adoring the presence of Buddha (Indian 2nd Cent. A.D.) *British Museum*	54
M	Bronze Head of a Young Woman, Benin City (16th Century) *British Museum*	61

12

ILLUSTRATIONS 5

N Part of a Painting on a small silken roll. Admonitions of 68
the instructress in the Palace, by the Ku K'ai-chih (364–
405 A.D.) *British Museum*
The heroism of the fair Fong (1st Century, B.C.) At a spectacle at which wild animals were exhibited a bear broke loose and rushed towards the Emperor; all the ladies present fled except Fong, stepped in the path of the bear that her death might divert its attack. Her sacrifice was prevented by spearmen of the Guard who ran up and dispatched the bear.

O Bronze Cat (Egyptian) *Collection Stoclet, Brussels* 75

Plate A

13   My master the celebrated Chang says: 'Having no leanings is called Chung, admitting of no change is called Yung. By Chung is denoted Equilibrium; Yung is the fixed principle regulating everything under heaven.'

14   What heaven has ordained is man's Nature; an accordance with this is the Path; the regulation of it is Instruction.

There is nothing more visible than what is secret – nothing more manifest than what is minute. The superior man is careful: he is but one.

When anger, sorrow, joy, pleasure are in being but are not manifested, the mind may be said to be in a state of Equilibrium; when the feelings are stirred and co-operate in due degree the mind may be said to be in a state of Harmony. Equilibrium is the great principle.

If both Equilibrium and Harmony exist everything will occupy its proper place and all things will be nourished and flourish.

From the *Chung Yung, The Doctrine of Equilibrium and Harmony*

THE FOUNDATIONS OF AESTHETICS

15 Many intelligent people give up aesthetic speculation and take no interest in discussions about the nature or object of Art, because they feel that there is little likelihood of arriving at any definite conclusion. Authorities appear to differ so widely in their judgements as to which things are beautiful, and when they do agree there is no means of knowing *what* they are agreeing about.

What in fact do they mean by Beauty? Professor Bosanquet and Dr Santayana, Signor Croce, and Clive Bell, not to mention Ruskin and Tolstoy, each in his own way dogmatic, enthusiastic, and voluminous, each leaves his conclusions equally uncorrelated with those of his predecessors. And the judgements of experts on one another are no less at variance. But if there is no reason to suppose that people are talking about the same thing, a lack of correlation in their remarks need not cause surprise. We assume too readily that similar language involves similar 16 thoughts and similar things thought of. Yet why should there be only one subject of investigation which has been called Aesthetics? Why not several fields to be separately investigated, whether they are found to be connected or not? Even a Man of Letters, given time, should see that if we say with the poet:

> 'Beauty is Truth, Truth Beauty' – that is all
> Ye know on earth, and all ye need to know.

we need not be talking about the same thing as the author who says:

> The hide of the rhinoceros may be admired for its fitness; but as it scarcely indicates vitality, it is deemed less beautiful than a skin which exhibits mutable effects of muscular elasticity.

What reason is there to suppose that one aesthetic doctrine can be framed to include all the valuable kinds of what is called Literature:

> All tongues speak of him, and the bleared sights
> Are spectacled to see him, your prattling nurse
> Into a rapture lets her baby cry
> While she chats him: the kitchen malkin pins
> Her richest lockram 'bout her reechy neck
> Clamb'ring the walls to eye him.

To this satire may be opposed the unsubstantial music of the following passage, yet both must take a high place in any account of literary values:

> Such a soft floating witchery of sound
> As twilight Elphins make, when they at eve
> Voyage on gentle gales from Fairyland,
> Where Melodies round honey-dropping flowers,
> Footless and wild, like birds of Paradise,
> Nor pause, nor perch, hovering on untam'd wing!

No one explanation seems sufficient to cover such a wide difference. It is not surprising therefore that aesthetic theories are equally different. Let us nevertheless attempt to make a classification.

Chapter One
AESTHETIC EXPERIENCES

Whenever we have any experience which might be called 'aesthetic', that is whenever we are enjoying, contemplating, admiring, or appreciating an object, there are plainly different parts of the situation on which emphasis can be laid. As we select one or other of these so we shall develop one or other of the main aesthetic doctrines. In this choice we shall, in fact, be deciding which of the main Types of Definition[1] we are employing. Thus we may begin with the object itself; or with other things such as Nature, Genius, Perfection, The Ideal, or Truth, to which it is related; or with its effects upon us. We may begin where we please, the important thing being that we should know and make clear which of these approaches it is that we are taking, for the objects with which we come to deal, the referents to which we refer, if we enter one field will not as a rule be the same as those in another. Few persons will be equally interested in all, but some acquaintance with them will at least make the interests of other people more intelligible, and discussion more profitable. Differences of opinion and differences of interest in these matters are closely interconnected, but any attempt at a general synthesis, premature perhaps at present, must begin by disentangling them. A third quotation essentially unlike either of those already given above may help to make this quite clear:

> By the waters of Babylon
> We sat down and wept:
> When we remembered thee, O Sion.
> As for our harps, we hanged them up:
> Upon the trees that are therein.
> For they that led us away captive required of us then a song,
> And melody in our heaviness:

---

[1] A full account of these will be found in Chapter 5 of *The Meaning of Meaning* (Kegan Paul, 1922) by the same authors.

> Sing us one of the songs of Sion.
> How shall we sing the Lord's song:
> In a strange land?
> If I forget thee, O Jerusalem:
> Let my right hand forget her cunning.
> If I do not remember thee,
> Let my tongue cleave to the roof of my mouth:
> Yea, if I prefer not Jerusalem in my mirth.
> Remember the Children of Edom, O Lord,
> In the day of Jerusalem:
> How they said, Down with it, down with it,
> Even to the ground.
> O daughter of Babylon, wasted with misery: 20
> Yea, happy shall he be that rewardeth thee,
> As thou hast served us.
> Blessed shall he be that taketh thy children: and
>   throweth them
> Against the stones.

We have then to make plain the method of Definition which we are employing. The range of useful methods is shown in the following table of definitions, most of which represent traditional doctrines, while others, not before emphasized, render the treatment approximately complete.

It should be borne in mind throughout this volume that anything judged to be beautiful is either a work of art or a natural object. A work of art may clearly *be regarded* in both ways, but not simultaneously. When we regard it as a work of art we take the attitude of the contemplator, our attitude, that is to say is modified by the preceding activity of another mind; but when we look at it as a natural object (as we *may* do in painting a cathedral) we take the attitude of an artist, that is to say, we make our own selection.

The Senses of Beauty

A {   I Anything is beautiful – which possesses the simple quality of Beauty.
    II Anything is beautiful – which has a specified Form.

21 B {
III Anything is beautiful – which is an imitation of Nature.
IV Anything is beautiful – which results from successful exploitation of a Medium.
V Anything is beautiful – which is the work of Genius.
VI Anything is beautiful – which reveals (1) Truth, (2) the Spirit of Nature, (3) the Ideal, (4) the Universal, (5) the Typical.[1]
VII Anything is beautiful – which produces Illusion.
VIII Anything is beautiful – which leads to desirable Social effects.

C {
IX Anything is beautiful – which is an Expression.
X Anything is beautiful – which causes Pleasure.
XI Anything is beautiful – which excites Emotions.
XII Anything is beautiful – which promotes a Specific emotion.
XIII Anything is beautiful – which involves the processes of Empathy.
XIV Anything is beautiful – which heightens Vitality.
XV Anything is beautiful – which brings us into touch with exceptional Personalities.
XVI Anything is beautiful – which conduces to Synaesthesis.

22   The fields reached by these various approaches can all be cultivated and most of them are associated with well known names in the Philosophy of Art.[2] Let us, however, suppose that we have selected one of these fields and cultivated it to the best of our ability ; for what reasons was it selected rather than some other ? For if we approach the subject in the spirit of a visitor to

---

1 Editorial Note: When first published in 'The Sense of Beauty' (1921) this list included a sixth item: 'the Fourth Dimension'.
2 As this discussion is throughout concerned with the theory of Beauty, we are not called upon to examine the various senses in which the word Art has also been used. Thus when we refer to Art in connection with e.g., Imitation, we are referring to beauty in anything that has generally been called Art as opposed to Nature.

the Zoo, who, knowing that all the creatures in a certain enclosure are 'reptiles', seeks for the common property which distinguishes them as a group from the fish in the Aquarium, mistakes may be made. We enter, for example, the Fitzwilliam Museum, and, assuming that all the objects there collected are beautiful, attempt similarly to establish some common property. A little consideration of how they came there might have raised serious doubts; but if, after the manner of many aestheticians, we persist, we may even make our discovery of some relevant common property appear plausible. Anyone, however, who, after a study of these and similar objects, wished to know why he should prefer one to another would find himself confronted by the possibilities we have set forth in our list.

Plate B

Plate C

Chapter Two
BEAUTY AS INTRINSIC

If the reader decides to admit, I, simple aesthetic properties,[1] such as beauty, loveliness, grandeur, and prettiness, and supposes that things have these properties as they have redness or temperature, he has the dictionary on his side, but gets no further enlightenment as to the nature of his experiences. Such an aesthetic, though capable of much elegant internal development, as, for example, the postulation of a special Sense of Beauty, has no connections with any other aspects of the Universe. Beauty becomes an ultimate unanalysable idea, and no criticism or discussion is possible. Such a view gains support from the existence of many works whose artistic value it has been difficult to explain by current theories (Plate C), or which have not generally been regarded as works of Art – e.g., aeroplanes, etc. If, on the other hand, he does not allow such properties and considers that what he is preferring is, II, some arrangement of physical features, he is committed to the view that one arrangement of physical features can be *in itself* preferable to (more valuable than) another. It is at least doubtful

---

[1] As an example of an able and considered statement of the case for an intrinsic quality we may refer to pp. 127–144 of Professor John Laird's *Study in Realism*. 'Human actions', concludes Professor Laird, are 'good or bad in a moral sense, a value or its opposite belongs to them in the same sense as redness belongs to a cherry. For similar reasons the values of beauty or its opposite belong to certain things in certain connections, just as objectively as any other qualities.' Sculpture such as that shown in Plate B, might lead theorists to conclusions of this kind.

For a view of the second type (i.e., objective beauty as certain relations, etc., in a physical complex), with which, as we shall see, Mr Roger Fry toys in his remarks about necessary relations, reference may be made to the contention by Professor Kirschman in the University of Toronto Psychological Studies: 'A picture is a surface (a part of our field of vision), consisting of smaller surfaces which differ in space relation (extension, shape, arrangement), light quality (colour-tone and saturation), light intensity. All properties which the picture as a whole or in its parts possess, must be reducible to qualities or relations of these small surfaces. Consequently, any quality attributed to the work of art or its parts must be capable of being expressed in terms of these five or six variables.'

whether there is any sense in speaking of a preference for (the value of) things other than mental states or experiences. When people say they prefer coffee to tea, they will, if questioned, generally admit that it is either one flavour which they prefer to another, or one set of mental effects; and if they tasted neither, nor had effects from either, the two potations would be indifferent. Our inquirer will, on these grounds, take a psychological view, unless he is attracted by one of the doctrines comprised under group B.

Chapter Three
IMITATION

25 Among these we find what is, perhaps, the most popular view that has ever been held, the view namely, III, that art is essentially Imitation, and that a picture or a poem is beautiful in proportion as what it successfully imitates or describes is beautiful.

> The artist wrought this loved Guitar,
> And taught it justly to reply,
> To all who question skilfully,
> In language gentle as its own,
> Whispering in enamoured tone
> Sweet oracles of woods and dells,
> And summer winds in sylvan cells;
> For it had learnt all harmonies
> Of the plains and of the skies,
> Of the forests and the mountains,
> And the many voiced fountains;
> The clearest echoes of the hills,
> The softest notes of falling rills,
> The melodies of birds and bees,
> The murmuring of summer seas,
> And pattering rain and breathing dew,
> And airs of evening; and it knew
> That seldom-heard mysterious sound,
> Which, driven in its diurnal round,
> As it floats through boundless day,
> Our world enkindles on its way.

26 The implication that the problem of the beautiful as such would merely have been shifted into the realm of nature is generally concealed by a use of language which seems to place the beauty in the imitation itself (cf. Plate D). Aristotle combines this view with the pleasure doctrine, urging that there is a special pleasure in recognition. With the advent of the camera, however, the unique function of the artist was challenged, and at the same time theological considerations no longer allowed a

certain merit to every picture *qua* replica of God's handiwork. Today the esteem felt for mimicry and imitation is perceptibly dwindling.

In this connection it may be mentioned that, as with Eastlake's elephant *infra,* those who regard sunsets, peacocks, roses, river-girls, and racehorses as specially beautiful are generally making what Lalo has described as 'an implicit, confused, or instinctive judgement of the more or less normal, healthy, and typical or more or less powerful and highly developed character of a being or object of a given kind'. As is well known, such judgements are readily confused with other ascriptions of beauty.

Plate D

Plate E

Chapter Four
THE MEDIUM

27 It is, however, interesting to consider what may be meant by the dictum of the studios that things should be drawn 'as they really look', and concurrently by Mr Clive Bell's contention that representation of any kind is always irrelevant in Art. Representation involves two things, what is represented and a Medium. Let us first consider the general problem of the medium and its use, approaching the question through the three divisions of our list, from each of which we naturally arrive at different conclusions.

For doctrines of Group A the question is without interest; how medium and use are connected in a work will not for them be necessarily relevant. The work has beauty or has not beauty in the one case, in the other it either is of a certain physical form or it is not.

With doctrines of Group B the case is much the same. An Imitationist pure would be forced to the position that the more
28 like the medium is to the matter of the object represented, the better. The pure theory of Imitation, however, is uncommon, being usually compounded either with Revelatory or with Psychological Doctrines. Revelatory theorists favour somewhat the view that the less like the two are the better, but are not greatly concerned and leave the matter to the Psychologists. Social Moralists only intervene in disguise, and Expressionists hold for a mystic undiscussable relation of fitness.

We are thus left with C, the Psychological Theories. Of these the pleasure view tends to come into conflict with the others. There are certain suitabilities which connect media with their employment in the following fashion: Every medium has as a material its own peculiar effect upon our impulses. Thus our feelings towards clay and iron, towards the organ and the piano, towards colloquial and ceremonial speech are entirely different. Now upon all hands it is agreed, that these peculiar impulses must not be neglected. Those who maintain the pleasure view tend, however, to give them a special place by holding that the proper connection between medium and employment is that the employment must give to these impulses as much free play as possible on the ground that the free play of any impulse is pleasurable. The artist, they say, must respect the character of his medium and exploit it (Plate E). It is even common to find the view maintained, IV, that Art *is* the exploitation of the Medium.[1]

Those who hold the other psychological doctrines differ in refusing to allow so simple a connection such importance. While not denying that it is more natural to do certain things with one medium and other things with another they yet agree in laying no particular stress on the gratification of this group of impulses. They point out that there are many other impulses involved and hold that the emotion, vitality, empathy, or equilibrium which they desiderate, may require adjustments between the sets of impulses due to the medium and to its use, very different from mere mutual accommodation.

> Apter they are through the eagerness of their affection, that maketh them, which way soever they take, diligent in drawing their husbands, children, servants, friends, and allies the same way; apter through that natural inclination unto pity, which breedeth in them a greater readiness than in men to be bountiful towards their preachers who suffer want; apter through sundry opportunities which they have to procure encouragement for their brethren; finally, apter through a singular delight which they take in giving very large and particular intelligence how all nearabout them stand affected as concerning the same cause.

Although the medium and its use are here adapted to one another, this accordance is not so simple as a mere mutual accommodation, and conversely this last may be present in perfection in works of no merit whatever.

What, however, is at the root of the advice given to young

---

1 Cf. Mr. Marriott in the recent Oxford Symposium on 'Mind and Medium in Art', *B.J. Psych.*, xi. 1 ('Art is primarily the characteristic use of tools and materials', etc.).

artists to forget what they think things look like and draw them as they actually see them, is best explicable from our ways of recognizing what we see. The exigencies of everyday life accustom us to selecting only those aspects of experience which have a permanent and practical use. We normally react to our surroundings in ways which are labelled and classified in language, as stereotyped names. Thus grass is green or death is the end of life. In order, however, to react freely before a subject we must endeavour to be as little influenced by our habitual selections and attitudes as possible, – and this in the interest of representation itself. Death is the end of life:

> Or is it only a sweet slumber
> Stealing o'er sensation,
> Which the breath of roseate morning
> Chaseth into darkness?

What has to be reproduced is what is affecting the artist and nothing else, nothing dragged from some other context or irrelevant experience. Thus men are often seen as though they had one leg, the other being in fact either invisible or irrelevant. But if any memory or convention or assumption that men must have two legs leads us to draw in a couple of lower limbs this will be actually to the detriment of our representation. We must not, however, say with Mr Clive Bell that the artist should 'bring nothing from life', no acquaintance with its emotions or its experiences.[1] This is not only to demand an impossibility, but also arbitrarily and unnecessarily to restrict the field of aesthetic experience. What Mr Clive Bell perhaps desires to recommend is the attitude above described, but (unfortunately for his view) in every visual act we unavoidably bring to bear much of our past experience. The artist selects in virtue of the impulses

---

[1] Delacroix, *Journal* Vol. III, p. 97, raises a similar question, which presents no difficulties – 'Si nous sommes faits pour trouver dans cette créature qui nous charme le genre d'attrait propre a nous captiver, comment expliquer que ces mêmes traits, ces mêmes grâces particulières, pourront nous laisser froids, quand nous les trouverons exprimées dans les tableaux ou les statues.'

which his past life has developed in him. When we look at his work we shall in many cases miss much that is essential unless we are able to react with similar impulses (Plate F). To do so is necessarily to involve our past life. If with Mr Bell we regard as irrelevant everything except colour, line, and form, we may lessen the danger of undesirable associations, but at the price of missing a vital element in the work of art. The dispute is a little academic, because, as remarked above, this attitude could never be achieved by man, bird, or beast. In most painting the representational element in its proper place has its own important function. In poetry this is more obvious.

> We twa hae run about the braes,
>   And pou'd the gowans fine;
> But we've wander'd mony a weary fitt,
>   Sin auld lang syne.
>
> We twa hae paidl'd in the burn,
>   Frae morning sun till dine;
> But seas between us braid hae roar'd
>   Sin auld lang syne.

While emphasizing the influence of past experience, we need not go so far as Lafcadio Hearn, who says: 'When there is perceived some objective comeliness faintly corresponding to certain outlines of the inherited ideal, at once a wave of emotion ancestral bathes the long darkened image... the sense-reflection of the living objective becomes temporarily blended with the subjective phantasm, – with the beautiful luminous ghost made of centillions of memories... And so the Riddle resolves itself as Memory.'[1] Such 'organic memory' is, however, equally involved (cf. p. 68 *infra*) in all our experience whether of Beauty or not.

---

[1] *Exotics and Retrospectives*, pp. 202, 206.

Plate F

Chapter Five
GENIUS

Another doctrine of Group B, concerns, V, Genius. The distinction between classes of objects in virtue of their origin is well-known in many scientific fields; and common objects also are often identified by this means. Thus when we refer to Madeira, we have in view certain wines grouped together as coming from that source; and so it has been supposed that we know a work of art or recognize beauty as the creation of a certain type of man.

Thus we find Professor Külpe in a lengthy discussion of 'The Conception and Classification of Art' (University of Toronto Studies, Vol. 2, 1907) taking as his starting point the definition, 'Art is the product of genius – according to Kant and Schopenhauer', and objecting that genius produces scientific work as well, and that in the productions of works of art, 'more modest talent than genius is also acknowledged'. Light on the nature of genius from this point of view is thrown by doctrines which appear in Bergsonian literature.[1]

33

---

[1] Thus in Ruge's *Henri Bergson: an Account of his Life and Philosophy*, we read, 'The more we are entangled in living the less truly we are able to see.... We hardly see the object itself; we are content to know the class to which it belongs. We are content; but from time to time by happy chance men are born who are not bound to the treadmill of practical life. When they see a thing they look at it for itself; and according to circumstances become painters or sculptors, musicians or poets. What the artist gives us is, in short, a more direct vision of reality.... Nature thus at long intervals, and as though unawares, reveals reality to certain privileged beings.' If from phraseology such as this we are led to the not unnatural conclusion that Art is whatever certain privileged beings produce, we have a means of recognizing art when we have decided who amongst us are privileged and who suffering from illusions; and the controversy is shifted into the realms of social psychology.

I hae a wife o' my ain
    I'll partake wi naebody,
I'll tak' cuckold frae nain,
    I'll gie cuckold to naebody.

I hae a penny to spend,
    There – thanks to naebody;
I hae naething to lend,
    I'll borrow frae naebody.

I am naebody's lord,
    I'll be slave to naebody :
I hae a guid braid sword,
    I'll tak dunts frae naebody.

I'll be merry and free,
    I'll be sad for naebody;
Naebody cares for me,
    I care for naebody.

Plate G

Chapter Six
TRUTH

The general method employed in this enquiry is nowhere more valuable than in the discussion of, VI, Revelation. By its aid we may free ourselves in part from the apparent conflicts which the phonetic and graphic overlaps of distinct vocabularies (i.e., the use of the same terms to mean different things) occasion. In all revelatory doctrines, we are concerned in one sense or another with Truth. The relevant definitions of truth are at least as varied as those of Beauty. They cannot be adequately discussed here; one such set of opinions providing sufficient mental exercise for one occasion, but a few broad distinctions may be noted without overstraining the attention.

Thus when Aristotle suggests that the artist besides imitating should also preserve the type and at the same time ennoble it his suggestion may be taken in many ways. Eastlake, for instance, understands that, 'The elephant with his objectionable legs and inexpressive hide, may still be supposed to be a very normal specimen and so worthy of imitation by the artist', which is one way of interpreting 'the universal', namely as the typical. And Rymer in objecting to Shakespeare's Iago: 'He would pass upon us a close, dissembling, false, insinuating rascal, instead of an open-hearted, frank, plain-dealing Souldier, a character constantly worn by them for some thousands of years in the World', provides another interpretation namely as the conventional. Thirdly, Croce remarks of the view that art is imitation, 'Now truth has been maintained or at least shadowed with these words, now error. More frequently, nothing definite has been thought. One of the legitimate scientific meanings occurs when imitation is understood as representation or intuition of nature, a form of knowledge [cf. Plate G]. And when this meaning has been understood, by placing in greater relief the spiritual character of the process, the other proposition becomes also legitimate; namely that art is the idealization or idealizing imitation of nature.'

> Hark, hark! the lark at heaven's gate sings,
> And Phoebus 'gins arise,
> His steeds to water at those springs
> On chaliced flowers that lies.

37 Yet other variants may be found in Matthew Arnold for whom commerce with certain forms of art seemed 'to make those who constantly practised it... like persons who have had a very weighty and impressive experience: more truly than others under the empire of facts, and more independent of the language current among those with whom they live'; and in Coleridge 'The artist must imitate that which is within the thing, that which is active through form and figure, and discourses to us by symbols, – the Naturgeist, or spirit of nature', elsewhere defining beauty as 'the subjection of matter to spirit so as to be transformed into a symbol, in and through which the spirit reveals itself'.

MYSTICISM

It is plain that such different views as these require separate handling. Matthew Arnold's observation may be postponed until we discuss the doctrine of equilibrium within which it will find both a place and an explanation. Let us here consider the only other of these five views which requires attention, namely that of Coleridge. Having been stated as a mystical view, it can evidently only appeal in this form to those who adopt the special attitudes involved.

38 One natural statement of the mystical doctrine involved would be as follows. A certain emotion has occurred in the contemplation of a work of art or of nature, which represents or symbolizes either a special selection, or else in the supreme case the whole of, the past experience of the individual. It enables us to think of a complete range of experience, and this range is regarded as a datum upon a different level from any of the data

provided by portions of that range, and capable of giving knowledge as to the nature of the universe which the partial data of everyday experience do not readily yield.

Those to whom such an idea appears extravagant will explain the peculiar character of the emotions in question by saying perhaps that they are associated with unrecalled events in past experience.

The view of the world of art as a better world into which we may escape from the drabness and dullness of the present has close affinities with some kinds of idealization.

> Then let the winds howl on! their harmony
> Shall henceforth be my music, and the night
> The sound shall temper with the owlets' cry,
> As I now hear them in the fading light
> Dim o'er the bird of darkness' native site,
> Answer each other on the Palatine,
> With their large eyes, all glistening grey and bright,
> And sailing pinions. Upon such a shrine
> What are our petty griefs? – let me not number mine.

Chapter Seven
ILLUSION

39 If, however, VII, Illusion, is brought forward as the end of art we have a view which can be discussed on its own merits. Those who admire imitation are already on the way to such a view, and a picture which is merely regarded as a substitute for what might actually be seen is producing an illusion. It is only a further step to demand that the illusion shall be one of a more exciting, more inaccessible, or more congenial environment than the ordinary. On this theory Art is 'the quickest way out of Manchester'; and one can 'lose oneself in a novel', or 'forget one's troubles at the play' as easily as in drink.

This preoccupation with art as a means of escape is probably the cause of the public's taking so little interest in any but certain forms of representative art. An elaborate attempt has been made by Konrad Lange to justify this theory of art on the ground that man has an instinct to self-deception, which the artist satisfies; the essence of aesthetic appreciation being conscious self-deception. To the satirist or misanthrope such a theory often makes an appeal.

Plate H

CHAPTER EIGHT
SOCIAL EFFECTS

40   We may next consider the peculiar group of, VIII, Uplift doctrines which have emerged from the industrious homes of the late Victorian moralists. Mr John Ruskin, in spite of his real taste, maintained in his *Oxford Lectures* that Fine Art has only three functions – Enforcing the religious sentiments of men, Perfecting their ethical state, and Doing them material service (Plate H). The two last of these were also stressed by William Morris, and the two first by Tolstoy; it is, however, curious that Tolstoy's *What is Art?* shows no evidence of acquaintance with the work of Ruskin.

Tolstoy's insistence that great art must appeal to mankind in general is not necessarily connected with his moralistic and less valuable contentions; and advocates of a People's Theatre (cf. Romain Rolland's criteria) often seem to confuse the issue. From the side of Uplift, on the other hand, Professor W. R. Lethaby for instance in the *Hibbert Journal*, considers that 'Art is best con-
41   ceived as beneficent Labour which blesses both him who gives and him who receives. Beauty is its evidence. Beauty is virtue in being.' Or as Mr Middleton Murry has it, in his *Evolution of an Intellectual* (p. 55), the artist is he who 'by the compelling rhythm of his own progress becomes more and more a vehicle of the spirit which is for ever wrestling with its own materiality,... he but guides the world to the achievement of its own design. He penetrates and seeks to identify himself with this timeless progress, in order that he may become as it were, the taproot of the spirit which is at work in the world he contemplates.'

Finally Mr Clutton-Brock in his *Essays on Art* (1919) hazards the definition that the beauty of art 'is always produced by the effort to accomplish the impossible, and what the artist knows to be impossible. Art is the expression of a certain attitude towards reality, an attitude of wonder and value, a recognition of something greater than man; and where that recognition is not, art dies.'

We may compare and contrast the aristocratic attitude:

> I see before me the Gladiator lie:
> He leans upon his hand – his manly brow
> Consents to death, but conquers agony,
> And his droop'd head sinks gradually low –
> And through his side the last drops, ebbing slow
> From the red gash, fall heavy, one by one,
> Like the first of a thunder-shower; and now
> The arena swims around him: he is gone,
> Ere ceased the inhuman shout which hail'd the wretch
>   who won.
> He heard it, but he heeded not his eyes
> Were with his heart, and that was far away.

42

Considered as a post-war phenomenon the chief function of the revival of gratulation and homiletic is presumably the promotion of comfortable feeling in the hearts of men of good will, and as such no doubt it has a certain value. Some of these formulations will be observed to have affinities with revelatory doctrines moralised[1] through modern Protestant influence, and in this connection may best be regarded as still-born poems.

---

1 Cf. Baudelaire, *Curiosités Esthetiques*, p. 327: 'Qu'ils moissonnent, qu'ils sèment, qu'ils fassent paître des vaches, qu'ils tondent des animaux, ils ont toujours l'air de dire: "Pauvres désherités de ce monde, c'est pourtant nous qui le fécondent! Nous accomplissons une mission, nous exerçons un sacerdoce." Au lieu d'extraire simplement la poésie naturelle de son sujet, M. Millet veut à tout prix y ajouter quelque chose. Dans leur monotone laideur, tous ces petits parias ont une pretention philosophique, melancolique et raphaélesque. Ce malheur, dans la peinture de M. Millet, gâte toutes les belles qualités qui attirent tout d'abord le regard vers lui.'

Chapter Nine
EXPRESSIONISM

43 The most widely quoted formulation of the, IX, Expressionist view of Art, is that of Croce.

For certain readers this doctrine has a peculiar glamour. Impressionable essayists, who do not often meet with serious argumentation in the course of their literary perusals, and romantic persons who long for release from the laborious process of discrimination, are wont to find satisfaction in synthetic philosophies of the spirit which achieve unhoped for unifications.

The keystone of Croce's method consists in a skilful application of the Law of Identity combined with a partial denial of the Law of Contradiction. Thus when Intuition is identified with Expression it may be asserted that all intuitions are expressed without any further necessity of proof. Then if Intuition – expression be identified with Art, it follows that all intuitions are works of art. Since this process consists simply in the judicious
44 interchange of these strict synonyms the irresistible sweep of Croce's argument meets with no obstacle, and a healthy air of vigorous ratiocination is engendered! But it may be objected that too many things become Art. To this Croce replies that this does not distress him because 'no one has ever been able to indicate in what the something more consists ... the limits of the expressions that are called Art as opposed to those that are vulgarly called "not Art" are empirical and impossible to define. If an epigram be art why not a single word?'

Why not? That is precisely the difficulty of every expressionist's view, and in being hypnotized by his doctrine into according aesthetic value to every single word (if a word is a work of art why not a comma, which expresses a distinct impression of a pause?). Signor Croce himself invites us to attend the obsequies of expressionism. In fact the conclusion of the whole matter is the same as the beginning. Something happens which has been called Art, and which we too rightly call Art. This *is* Art.

As there is no reason to doubt his sincerity, and as his literary, dramatic, and historical writings are of such undoubted value, the most charitable explanation of this equivocation would be that Croce, preoccupied with the metaphysics of creative idealism, is endeavouring to say in speculative language something exceptionally obvious – for which he has attempted to create a personal vocabulary by exploiting the suggestive powers of accepted phrases.[1]

ECLECTICISM

Though it is less easy to extract a definite theory from the phraseology of Dr Bosanquet than from that of Croce, he may probably be regarded as an expressionist, though he wisely differs from Croce in objecting to the use made of intuition. In the *History of Aesthetic* we are given the Definition of Beauty, viz.: 'That which has characteristic or individual expression for sense-perception or imagination, subject to the conditions of general or abstract expressiveness in the same medium.' What-

---

1 With some confidence, then, it may be claimed, that Croce's English interpreters – such as Mr Carritt, who states, on p. 281 of *The Theory of Beauty*, 'a greater amount of truth is contained in Croce's *Estetica* than in any other philosophy of beauty that I have read', or the Reverend S. A. McDowall, who tells us on p. 18 of his *Beauty and the Beast* that 'It has been left for Croce to formulate the first satisfactory concept of beauty' – are too easily satisfied by rhetorical solutions. Mr Carritt, himself declares, 'My reading of Croce has convinced me that the *expression* of any feeling is beautiful.... All beauty is the expression of what may be generally called emotion, and all such expression is beautiful'; but almost in the same breath (p. 298) he goes on to admit that the only sort of expression which can 'strictly be called beautiful' is 'a particular way in which at a given moment any individual expresses himself.' We are left seeking further light on the particular way; and even the most piously erotic will hardly be better satisfied with Mr McDowall's improvement on his master – 'Mainly out of the relationship of sex, spring music, art, literature.... Croce missed the goal because he did not perceive that the content of Reality is relationship. God is Love; Reality is Love. Love is relationship. Beauty is the expression of an understanding of that relationship. Matter is beautiful because it is understood as the infinite activity of the spirit of love.' 'Matter' says Professor Eddington (*Space, Time and Gravitation*, p. 91), 'is built of electrons or other nuclei', and if his theory is to be truly all-embracing Mr McDowall should surely have said a word about the *libido* of the other nuclei, which are so infinitely active.

EXPRESSIONISM 39

ever else may be extracted from these cryptic words we at least seem to be concerned primarily with an Expressionist theory, and in *Lectures on Aesthetic*, p. 33, we read 'to say that the aesthetic attitude is an attitude of expression, contains, I believe, if rightly understood the whole truth of the matter'. But unlike Croce, Bosanquet is always toying with the hedonic alternative – as if uncertain what part pleasure should play. Thus in the *Lectures*, he describes the aesthetic attitude as 'preoccupation with a pleasant feeling, embodied in an object which can be contemplated ... there is probably some trace of the aesthetic attitude in almost all pleasant feeling.' We also learn (p. 103) that pleasantness is not 'a condition precedent of beauty; rather beauty is a condition precedent of pleasantness', while elsewhere (*History of Aesthetic*, p. 6), we note that 'things are not beautiful simply because they give pleasure, but only in so far as they give aesthetic pleasure'. Our suspicions are not allayed by the dictum 'Beauty is feeling become plastic', nor by this on the nature of ugliness – 'Suppose the beautiful silky ear of a dachshund replacing the ear of a beautiful human face.... Here we have in principle, I think, a genuine case of ugliness' (*Lectures*, p. 102).

It is time, however, to turn from such inconsequent, if suggestive, eclecticism[1] to doctrines falling definitely within the

---

1 We shall have occasion to note in relation to Empathy, that it is easy for anyone who is not clear as to the question he is endeavouring to answer to hover between several views according to the interest or context with which he is momentarily concerned. Thus one of the most informative of modern aestheticians, whose death at the age of 33 prevented his attaining that synthesis of which his learning and catholicity gave hope, Marie Jean Guyau, speaks of Art (which in *L'Irréligion de l'avenir* he regards as gradually taking the place of religion) for the most part after the manner of George Eliot, who regarded it as 'a mode of amplifying experience and extending our contact with our fellow-men beyond the bounds of our personal lot' (Type XV). The highest end of art, we read, is 'to produce an aesthetic emotion of a social character', *de produire une émotion esthétique d'un caractère social* (Type VIII); yet four pages earlier (*L'art au point de vue sociologique* (p.17)), he gives us a definition which, quoted in isolation as Professor Ross quotes it in his *Social Control*, p. 258, might be taken for an adumbration of the doctrine of equilibrium to which we shall return later (Type XVI). Art then appears

psychological field[1] which includes the third main group of theories.

Psychological Views

The definition of Art in terms of psychological effect came particularly into prominence with the evolutionary theories of the seventies which occupied themselves chiefly in discovering the survival value in everything which had succeeded in making good its right to survive. The evolutionists of those days regarded pleasure as a feeling which could be correlated with physiological function, and since Art seemed a form of activity with little apparent utility it was considered wise to relate it closely to Play which (*vide* kittens) involved the very practical idea of Exercise. Various continuations were then possible. The first

---

as 'an *ensemble* of means of producing that general and harmonious stimulation of the conscious life which constitutes the sentiment of the beautiful'. And when we turn *to L'esthétique contemporaine* for light on the difficulty, we get a third story (p. 77), this time purely hedonic. 'Beauty can, as I think, be defined thus: it is a perception or an action which stimulates in us life in all its three forms of sensibility, intelligence, and will at once, and produces pleasure by the rapid consciousness of this general stimulation ... *l'agréable est le fond même du beau*' (Type X) . When we add that Guyau found in play 'l'art dramatique à son premier degré' (in reply to Grant Allen) and held that 'Le type de l'émotion esthétique est l'émotion de l'amour. La beauté supérieure est la beauté feminine', it is hardly surprising to find M. Alfred Fouillée extracting from the works of his friend a Bergsonian doctrine of Art as 'almost synonymous with universal sympathy', as that which 'consiste à saisir et à rendre l'esprit des choses', by breaking down the barriers of the ego and 'uniting the individual with the all, and every portion of time with the whole of duration' (Type VI).

1 A subtle question is often raised here, namely, what it is which is to be called beautiful on these psychological views. Professor John Laird (*Realism*, p. 134), who, as we have noted, argues for the intrinsic view (Type I), contends that beauty is a predicate which 'cannot hold of anything less than the whole complex thing-that-is-felt-with-delight'; and Professor Alexander, whose general attitude would seem to have been largely determined by the perusal of Bosanquet, remarks (*Space, Time, Deity*, Vol. II, p. 294) that 'beauty belongs to the complex of mind and its object, to the beautiful object as expressed by the mind'. Such formulations are clearly relevant; and if we do not know whether we are applying the term beauty to the effect, to the cause, or to both together, purely verbal discussions, due to the Utraquistic Fallacy, will arise.

adopted by Herbert Spencer, saw in Play[1] and in Art a method of harmlessly expending superfluous energy. The faculties are as it were taken out for a trot lest they should atrophy or kick the stall down; and since the pleasure we get from arrangements of sounds and colours appeared unconnected with any vital function, Spencer was able to regard Art and the contemplation of works of Art as a refined sort of game, an enjoyment *de luxe*, its special differentia being its absolute divorce from utility (Plate I). This sort of treatment became known, and still is known, on the continent as the 'English aesthetic',[2] partly because the Darwinian movement was already associated with

---

1 Though the relations of Art and Play are frequently discussed in the literature of Aesthetics (cf. *infra* p. 90), it has not been considered necessary to examine as independent contributions the views of those who put forward either a Play-theory or a Sex-theory of Art. The instincts of Sex, no less than those of Play, are no doubt connected in various ways with aesthetics, but few have as yet committed themselves to the absurdities involved in constructing a definition of Beauty on the basis of such connections. We may recall, however, the opinion of Haydon (*Lectures on Painting and Design*, 1846, p. 258), that the Beautiful 'has its origin altogether in woman', and similar monstrosities may be found scattered throughout Phallic and Freudian literature. The fondness of writers like Mr Edward Carpenter (e.g., *The Art of Creation*, p. 188) for syntheses involving Beauty, Love, and the World-soul (cf. the language of Mr McDowall *supra*, p. 81) has helped to popularize such considerations.

2 'Aesthetic Pleasure', according to Grant Allen, p. 34, 'is the subjective concomitant of the normal amount of activity, not directly connected with life serving function, in the peripheral end organs of the cerebro-spinal nervous system' – the *passive* organs, whereas Play is the exercise of the *active* portion of our organism. 'What Play is to the active faculties, Art and the Aesthetic Pleasures are to the passive.'

Apart from the fact that Dancing is thus ruled out of the aesthetic field, the only further comment which need be made is the following extract from page 233 of Grant Allen's work, in which he voices a corollary of the pleasure-theory and the aesthetic requirements of his generation:

> We demand that a painter should choose for his theme beautifully-shaped objects, such as human figures, male or female, in graceful attitudes, nude and exquisitely formed, with rounded limbs, or clothed in flowing drapery, Greek or Roman, Oriental or Florentine; animals like the fawn, the panther, the Arab charger, the swan, and the butterfly; mountain peaks, bossy hills, winding bays; the cataract leaping in an arch from the crag; Naples and Vesuvius and Niagara, the curved horizon of ocean, the thousand inlets of a highland loch; graceful pottery, elegantly-moulded goblets, flagons, and vases, slender beakers and shapely chalices; the domes and minarets of Stamboul, the sweeping arches of Tintern and Poitiers, the columns of Paestum, the rounded tiers and galleries of the amphitheatre. On the other hand, the painter

42   FOUNDATIONS OF AESTHETICS

these islands, and partly because the only English contribution to the theory of Aesthetics widely read on the continent in the century and a half which elapsed between Hogarth's *Analysis of Beauty* and the essays of Vernon Lee and Clive Bell is Grant Allen's *Physiological Aesthetics*.

avoids (except for some special effect of colour or contrast) lean, harsh, and angular limbs or features, constrained and graceless clothing, awkward postures and actions; heavy, ungainly, or shapeless animal forms, such as the bear, the cart-horse, the goose, and the slug; flat monotonous plains; the still ocean unbroken by a winding shore or bluff headland, unrelieved by a ship with bellied sails or a tempest curling the breakers on the beach; straight streets, plain rectangular houses, square windows, and flat façades destitute of arch or column, dome or portico.

To careful students of Burlington House it will come as no surprise to learn that in landscape painting 'the choice of "bits" is one of the greatest tests of an artist's natural taste. Autumn and sunset are the chosen seasons of the painter as well as the poet.' And finally 'I have seen at least one painting of a throstle in a hawthorn bush, pouring forth its soul in open-mouthed delight, so that the very notes of its song trembled in one's ear' – or as Dr Johnson might have said, 'I have seen at least one painting of Scottish scenery in which, Sir, the road to England was so perspicuously delineated that the very traffic of Fleet Street roared in my delighted ear.'

Plate I

Plate J

Chapter Ten
PLEASURE

52 To take the most accomplished modern advocate of, X, the theory of Beauty, as pleasure – 'Beauty', says Dr Santayana, is 'pleasure regarded as a quality of a thing'. All pleasures are intrinsic and positive values, and beauty is constituted by the objectification of pleasure (Plate J).

Once upon a time, the story runs, we thus objectified all our experiences, and thought that whatever happened to us had happened to things around us. But 'modern philosophy has taught us to say the same thing of every element of the perceived world; all are sensations; and their grouping into objects imagined to be permanent and external is the work of certain habits of our intelligence'.

In order to get a sense of Beauty therefore, we have to commit a 'radically absurd fallacy'. But since though recognizing it as such, we can go on committing it, this doctrine is not quite self-destructive, and those who are interested can examine the conditions under which we perform so curious and interesting an operation. We shall return to the question of objectification, or projection, in connection with the *Einfühlung* theory, and we shall also have occasion to notice that pleasure is assigned a sub-
53 ordinate place in most aesthetic doctrines, sometimes a necessary, more often a mere adventitious place. Meanwhile, there is no doubt that many people do use the term Beauty as a synonym for being the cause of pleasure, and the hedonist can be left to exploit his own field – the study of the things which please humanity – without interfering with others who have equally interesting work in hand.

The disadvantage of a pleasure view is that it offers us too restricted a vocabulary. We need fuller terms with which to describe the value of works of art.

It is a beauteous evening, calm and free,

The holy time is quiet as a nun
Breathless with adoration; the broad sun
Is sinking down in its tranquillity;
The gentleness of heaven broods o'er the sea.
Listen! the mighty being is awake,
And doth with his eternal motion make
A sound like thunder everlastingly.
Dear child! dear girl! that walkest with me here,
If thou appear untouched by solemn thought,
Thy nature is not therefore less divine:
Thou liest in Abraham's bosom all the year;
And worshipp'st at the temple's inner shrine,
God being with thee when we know it not.

Chapter Eleven
EMOTION

54 Let us next examine the claims of the Emotionalist. Works of art, it has been held, are those works which are produced under stress of emotion. The first consequence of such a view is that war poetry, the poetry of school-girls, and not a little religious verse is thereby rendered an object of serious interest. If, instead, we chose as works of art those objects which, XI, evoke some emotion in their beholders, we have (Dentists' Drills) a similarly heterogeneous collection of stimulants, with no particular reason adduced why emotion is held to be desirable. If it is said that Art is what causes desirable emotions we find ourselves again in the familiar field of the moralist.

Without, however, bringing in moral considerations there are some emotions which have value, and which works of art can impart (Plate K). It is clear that this view covers many works of a high order in which consistency of emotional sequence is the ruling principle.

55
    He is gone on the mountain,
        He is lost to the forest,
    Like a summer-dried fountain,
        When our need was the sorest.
    The font, reappearing
        From the raindrops shall borrow,
    But to us comes no cheering,
        To Duncan no morrow!

    The hand of the reaper
        Takes the ears that are hoary,
    But the voice of the weeper
        Wails manhood in glory.
    The autumn winds rushing
        Waft the leaves that are serest,
    But our flower was in flushing,
        When blighting was nearest.

> Fleet foot on the correi,
>   Sage council in cumber,
> Red hand in the foray,
>   How sound is thy slumber!
> Like the dew on the mountain,
>   Like the foam on the river,
> Like the bubble on the fountain,
>   Thou art gone, and for ever!

It will be admitted that emotional art merits the wide attention which it receives, and if (as in the case of Millet and Rembrandt, Tchaikovsky, and Strauss) the emotions are refined and developed and general participation is made possible, it gains additional value.

But it is not easy to ascribe the highest value to emotions in general, merely as emotions. They may often be experienced without particular significance, and have their place without necessarily being the concern of art. For these reasons most writers who have advanced the emotionalist theory have felt constrained to narrow the field to, XII, some unique emotion. Introspective analysis, however, has not convinced psychologists that the postulated emotion can be admitted. It is not otherwise known, has never been described, and is much in need of identification.

Plate K

Chapter Twelve
SIGNIFICANT FORM

Failing some non-circular method of describing such an emotion, no field of enquiry emerges.[1] Some however of the incidental remarks by which this doctrine is supported in what is the best known of recent expositions deserve attention.

Mr Clive Bell begins by defining 'works of art' as 'the objects that provoke a peculiar emotion (aesthetic emotion)'. So far all is well. He poses next, as 'the central problem of aesthetics', the discovery of 'some quality common and peculiar to all the objects that provoke this emotion'. Now this, as our analysis will show, is a purely artificial question due to superstitions about causes and effects. No such common and peculiar quality can reasonably be looked for, if we start from Mr Clive Bell's starting point. The 'central problem' he proposes to solve does not arise.

His reason for this divagation is given on the same page; 'either all works of visual art have some common quality, or when we speak of "works of art" we gibber'. This is true, but the

---

[1] Attempts to bring order into our treatment of such elusive experiences as that of Beauty are always liable to misunderstanding, and to criticism by those who are suspicious of 'theory', or concern themselves exclusively with appreciation or creative work. Sometimes this mistrust is due to a preference for 'evocative' language where questions of feeling and appreciation are concerned, and to this we refer later. But artists or musicians are also commonly supposed to resent what they regard as an endeavour to label, and by implication limit, the 'life of the spirit' – to define, as the phrase goes, what is essentially 'indefinable'. To any such resentment we could only reply that it would have been based on a misinterpretation of our purpose. If what is regarded as the essential in such experiences seems neither to fall into one of the groups in which we have arranged the judgements of the past and of the present, nor to be covered by some obvious combination of these, nothing that is said here would conflict with the addition to the list of further descriptions. Even to those who doubt the possibility of an authentic description, the knowledge of what has actually been said or thought on any subject is seldom without value. And a conviction that the vocabulary of 'Pleasure' or 'Expression' or 'Emotion' is inadequate to the description sought may lead to the consideration of other mental states and to a better understanding of these – if not to the conclusion which is suggested below that the imagined *impasse* was due to a wrong orientation, rather than to the deficiencies of language or the baffling complexity of the subject.

required quality is already to hand in his definition. When we speak of 'works of art' we understand 'objects which provoke aesthetic emotion'. So far as this argument goes, there is no reason whatever to go seeking for further points of agreement.[1]

Which explains why Mr Clive Bell's second definition of

---

[1] But it may be said 'If certain objects agree in producing in us a peculiar effect (aesthetic emotion) is not this fact a ground for supposing that there must be something common and peculiar in them to which this effect is due?' The plausibility of this fallacy is well known and it is clear that Mr Clive Bell has been victimized. That it is a fallacy becomes plain when we consider a few analogous cases. Thus of all the things which cause death we can say, if we like, that they are lethal, but we are no longer tempted to think that we are saying anything more about them than that death did occur in connection with them. We no longer taboo them on the ground that they must necessarily have something deathly within them. Similarly with pleasing things, or with things which hurt, or with frightening things. More evidently still with beautiful things.

The way in which the fallacy comes to seem plausible is best shown by taking a case in which we can make our statements more precise. We may admit that things which hurt need have no common quality, but still hold that if we narrow down the kind of pain produced we shall be able then to find a common peculiar quality in the things which cause it. Thus the pain of being burnt we shall say implies heat, and the pain of being cut implies sharpness, and similarly the effect produced by a work of art (aesthetic emotion) implies a common peculiar quality in works of art.

But at this point in our narrowing down we automatically beg the question. What we refer to by 'the common peculiar quality' is nothing different from the character of the effect we notice. We are simply grammatically translating a description of an effect which we experience into a description of the most prominent object connected with the effect. We do not say any more by this procedure. 'That causes me aesthetic emotion' and 'That has a peculiar quality such that I have aesthetic emotion before it' are identical assertions, *if our sole ground for the second is the first*. For purposes of writing and speech the alternative locution is convenient when those who use it know what they are doing. But we must be able to distinguish the cases where we know independently both common qualities of causes and common qualities of effects (and so can set about observing their connections), from those cases where we only know common qualities of effects and try from these to infer common qualities in their causes. In the first case we have something to investigate. In the second case we are limited to grammatical tricks with our symbols.

If this point of view be accepted, and in addition if the search for '*the* meaning of Beauty' be abandoned in favour of the procedure here advocated, it will be clear that what is regarded as important in one treatment may be neglected in another. It follows, therefore, that though a philosopher or critic may have been 'wrong' in the 'solution' he has put forward (the field he has selected), he may, as we frequently have occasion to point out, have made valuable remarks on matters which, for his purposes, appeared to be of secondary interest. And further verbal differences, due to his philosophic system, may conceal a real agreement, which translation or regrouping would serve to reveal.

Significant Form as 'aesthetically moving form' has seemed to some people to carry the matter very little further; and also why he sets out with such confidence to show that what moves me, moves me, i.e., 'to show that significant form is the only quality common and peculiar to all the works of visual art that move me' (p. 10). He is too modest, however, in describing this arrangement of words as an hypothesis. There is no reason to suppose that there must be some one quality without which a work of art cannot exist (p. 7), particularly for an author who especially asserts (p. 8), that 'we have no other means of recognizing a work of art than our feeling for it'.

None the less, the phrase 'significant form' seems to exercise a hypnotic influence. Mr Roger Fry, for example, whose earlier view, as published in the *New Quarterly* in 1909, was that Beauty is what arouses ordered emotion satisfying to the imaginative life (i.e., a straightforward emotionalist theory of Type XI) is amongst those who have succumbed. In his recently published *Vision and Design* (p. 195) he says: 'Some artists who were peculiarly sensitive to the formal relations of works of art had almost no sense of the emotions which I had supposed them to convey... It became evident that I had not pushed the analysis of works of art far enough.' And he finally enumerates as amongst the questions of aesthetics which remain to be solved the nature of 'significant form' and what is the value of this elusive – and taking the whole mass of mankind – rather uncommon emotion which it causes'. As in the case of his excursions into logic ('The specifically aesthetic emotion by means of which the necessity of relations is apprehended, and which corresponds in science to the purely logical process.' *Athenæum*, 1919), Mr Fry is unfortunate when he ceases to rely on his own judgement.

The method of approach here employed is one which involves certain deviations from accepted groupings and terminology; but that deviation is not such that intelligibility would be increased by the creation of a new vocabulary, nor is it greater than that caused in the case of others by their difference of outlook, for which we have endeavoured, on all occasions, to allow.

The state of mind which he and Mr Clive Bell discuss *may* be what will later be described[1] in connection with Synaesthesis, and, if so, we shall avoid the tacitly anti-Tolstoyan[2] view that
62 Beauty is only for a select few who are endowed with the faculty of recognizing this esoteric entity.

> ... lo in these hours supreme,
> No poem proud, I chanting bring to thee, nor mastery's rapturous verse,
> But a cluster containing night's darkness and blood-dripping wounds,
> And psalms of the dead.

---

1 It is necessary to bear in mind the distinction between the evocative and the scientific use of language. Evocative language which is employed primarily to produce effects by suggestion, may (as is obvious in all poetry) be highly misleading if interpreted as though it had a scientific function. Thus the phrase 'Significant form', meaningless if we ask logically 'significant of what?' may be of value in giving the mind a certain direction, which may help to account for its appeal to certain readers.

2 It is odd that Mr Fry (p. 193) attaches so much importance to Tolstoy's least original tenet. That art is the *communication* of something may be regarded as common ground to all aesthetics (cf. even Coleridge's mockery of the novel: 'A sort of mental *camera obscura* manufactured at the printing office which *pro tempore* fixes, reflects, and transmits the moving phantasms of one man's delirium, so as to people the barrenness of a hundred other brains afflicted with the same trance.' – *Biographia Literaria*, Chapter 3). Tolstoy's originality lay chiefly in his insistence on *universality* as a test of great art – the width of the appeal; he had no historical acquaintance with aesthetics and relied chiefly on the paraphrases in Knight's uncritical compilation.

Plate L

Chapter Thirteen
EMPATHY

63 It remains conceivable, that a work of art should have some one quality in virtue of which we recognize it as such, though there are very strong general reasons against the assumption. It is plain that a description of what happens when we feel aesthetic emotion (if ever we do) would fall into two halves. There would be a long psychological story about the organization of our impulses and instincts and of the special momentary setting of them due to our environment and our immediate past history on the one hand. On the other a physico-physiological account of the work of art as a stimulus, describing also its immediate sensory effects, and the impulses which these bring into play. The responsibility for the aesthetic emotion which results must be shared among all these factors. Even if we can detect some of the more important factors in the psychological conditions and group them as constant, as we seem to do when we talk of 'sensitive persons', we are still left with a very complicated set of conditions.

64
>O gentle sleep!
>Nature's soft nurse, how have I frighted thee,
>That thou no more wilt weigh my eyelids down,
>And steep my senses in forgetfulness?
>Why rather, sleep, liest thou in smoky cribs
>Upon uneasy pallets stretching thee,
>And hushed with buzzing night-flies to thy slumber,
>Than in the perfumed chambers of the great,
>Under the canopies of costly state,
>And lulled with sounds of sweetest melody?
>O thou dull god! Why liest thou with the vile,
>In loathsome beds, and leav'st the kingly couch,
>A watch-case, or a common 'larum bell?
>Wilt thou upon the high and giddy mast
>Seal up the ship-boy's eyes, and rock his brains
>In cradle of the rude imperious surge,

> And in the visitation of the winds,
> Who take the ruffian billows by the top,
> Curling their monstrous heads and hanging them
> With deaf'ning clamours in the slippery clouds,
> That, with the hurly, death itself awakes?
> Can'st thou, O partial sleep! give thy repose
> To the wet sea-boy in an hour so rude;
> And in the calmest and most stillest night,
> With all appliances and means to boot,
> Deny it to a king?

Let us but attempt to realize what is involved here! The likelihood that there is any one condition which is essential grows the smaller, the more we realize what the degree of this complexity must be. There is good reason to deny that emotion is ever the result of the stimulation merely of one impulse. It seems to be due always to the interaction of many. A long psychological investigation opens here. One branch of this, explored with great care by Lipps, has in the natural course of such things been transformed into an aesthetic. This is XIII, Empathy.

It is well known that we are supposed to ascribe movement to lines and shapes which in themselves are essentially stationary, just as we ascribe body to pictorial surfaces. The doctrine of *Einfühlung* or Empathy advocated by Lipps, is an attempt to explain this phenomenon. Lotze in his *Mikrokosmos* remarked on the way in which we 'project ourselves into the forms of a tree, identifying our life with that of the slender shoots which swell and stretch forth, feeling in our souls the delight of the branches which drop and poise delicately in mid-air. We extend equally to lifeless things these feelings which lend them meaning' (Plate L). Almost any illustration from poetry will make this point plain. And by such feelings we transform the inert masses of a building into so many limbs of a living body, a body experiencing inner strains which we transport back in ourselves. 'We have', said Souriau (*Esthètique du mouvement*, 1889) a quarter of a century later 'only one way of imagining things from inside, and that is putting ourselves inside them'.

Forms, says Lipps, arise in reality under specified mechanical conditions, to which we give the name of forces. What we call the rhythm of poetry, again, is a rhythm of the acts of perceiving the accentuated and un-accentuated or less accentuated syllables. And since rhythm is universal in character, any psychical process can become the vehicle thereof, with a result that we get a sympathetic vibration of the whole personality, a connecting rhythm and mood.

> And the invisible rain did ever sing
> A silver music on the mossy lawn.

So the qualities which we attribute (as we attribute to other things frightfulness, novelty, and quaintness) to rhythms, sounds, and colours (seriousness and cheerfulness: fullness and quietness: warmth and depth) are not heard and seen, but denote the manner in which we are internally moved when sounds and colours are being perceived.

> The pillowy silkiness that rests
> Full in the speculation of the stars.

Aesthetic pleasure, Lipps concluded, is 'dependent upon the attribution of life', and aesthetic contemplation always involves such attributes. Space, for example, is an object of aesthetic perception 'only inasmuch as it is a space which has been given life', and is thus the vehicle of inner tension; and it is the mission of the arts of beautiful spatial form to increase this interchange of activities and to diversify it. Here, with the addition of a few stray dicta about 'meaningful rhythms of living', Lipps concludes his account, leaving it to others to develop out of such considerations any more definite approximation to an aesthetic. And independently, or under the influence of his analysis, these others have not been wanting.[1]

---

[1] Says Berenson, *Tuscan Painters*, p. 84, 'The more we endow an object with human attributes, the less we merely know, and the more we realize it, the more does it approach the work of art', and we find those who approach the same question from the

The only reason which prevents such accounts of empathic processes being formulated as a complete aesthetic theory, is the uncertainty of their authors as to what sort of answers may be expected to the question 'What is Beauty?' For all these accounts introduce at the critical point some implication as to 'pleasure' or 'harmony' or to both of these, in such a way as to leave it open whether their discussion has not merely been concerned with a part of the machinery of appreciation in general.

Vernon Lee's elaborate summary of the whole controversy is at once the clearest indication of this uncertainty, and the most confused in its ultimate conclusions. Referring to the place of memory in the story, she remarks (*Beauty and Ugliness*, p. 21): 'The projection of an experience into the non-ego involves the more or less vivid revival of that experience in ourselves; and that revival, according to its degree of vividness, is subject to the same accompaniment of satisfaction or dissatisfaction as the original experience. So when this attribution of our modes of life to visible shapes and this revival of past experience is such as to be favourable to our existence and in so far pleasurable, we welcome the form thus animated by ourselves as "beautiful".' Hence, she concludes, 'Empathy has conditioned the being of art and can explain it'. We could hardly ask more of a Theory of Beauty. We have, it appears, a defining judgement to enable us to distinguish which projections are beautiful, and an account of projections and their stimulation which enables us to differentiate the class of objects that can act as stimuli.

Thus:

1. Not all objects, but those into which we can project movement correlated with a peculiar dynamical experience in ourselves, are aesthetic.

---

standpoint of psychological theory finding the whole solution in the field of empathic processes. 'If the energies which we feel in the lines are external projections of our own energies', says Münsterberg, 'We understand the psychological reasons why certain combinations of lines please us and others do not. They ought to be such that they correspond to the natural energies of our own organism and represent the harmony of our own muscular functions.'

2. Not all such objects are beautiful, but those which cause pleasure, because they facilitate our vitality (cf. Plate M).

> I hear a springing water, whose quick sound
> Makes softer the soft sunless patient air.

In the light of our previous remarks, however, the claim has only to be stated for its weakness to become apparent. In the first place, unless it is deliberately to be interpreted as differing from the doctrine of pleasure, we have merely that doctrine stated in a vaguer form and over a more limited range. Secondly, the experiences we get from successfully riding a bicycle, which presumably cause pleasure and facilitate our vitality, could clearly be recalled by our projecting similar movements into lines and rhythms, and the resultant state would be neither more nor less aesthetic than the original one, except in virtue of its new origin in recall through projection. And such an origin is hardly more relevant to aesthetics than if the same state were to be recalled by internal stimuli in a dream.

70   This does not mean that it would be impossible to find fields which on such principles could be labelled 'Aesthetics' by an enthusiastic empathist *pur sang*, but since no one not misled by terminology has yet marked out such a field *qua* aesthetician, it is hardly worth while to set up and overturn dummies for hypothetical monomaniacs.

As regards the general nature of Empathy as part of the process of appreciation, we may note that the terminology in which it has been described has itself misled even the ablest writers on the subject. The treachery of the term *Einfühlung*, as used by Professor Lipps, has been well indicated by Vernon Lee. In its reflexive form it implies that the ego or *personality* in some sense goes over into the object, and is merged therein, so that Lipps contended that if Empathy was in progress, we could not be aware of the inner imitation or muscular movements which (in the similar view of Groos) accompany the process.

The importance of this sort of consideration lies in its bearing on the 'impersonal' attitude which is regarded by many as the essential of aesthetic contemplation.

Whatever the importance of empathic phenomena when correctly described in showing us how we come to speak of certain objects as we do, it should be clear that they do not provide a consistent theory of Beauty in the same way that the hedonic theory does; though an empathic theory has been verbally formulated by some of its advocates so as to lead them to suppose that an aesthetic had been involved. Moreover, there is undoubtedly a sense in which certain relations of formal symmetry, a certain distribution of weight, the even interplay of qualities and intensities, may lead to a mere judgement of balance on the perceptual level, the balance being usually judged to be in the work of art. Where undue importance is claimed for this type of judgement, inadequate theories tend to arise, which narrow the application of the term *balance*, although such superficial balances may create a predisposition towards the more important forms of appreciation with which we are about to deal.

Throughout the discussion of empathy, with its account of the initiation of impulses, and its glances at the physiology and psychology of certain elementary forms of balance, we find ourselves constantly approaching or entering the field which our enquiry had reached when the claims of the emotionalist had engaged attention.

Plate M

Chapter Fourteen
SYNAESTHESIS

It remains only to formulate, XVI, a doctrine which seems essentially that to be attributed to Confucius in the quotations from the *Chung Yung* at the head of this book. In doing so we shall be enabled to place in their true position the two remaining definitions on our list. It is expected that the experience now about to be described will be recognized by those who look for it; it has, indeed, been noticed by many poets and critics. It marks off a field which cannot otherwise be defined and also explains why the objects therein contained can reasonably be regarded as of great importance. The limits of this field do not correspond with those set by a naïve use of the term Beauty, but it will be found that the actual usage of careful and sensitive persons not affected by special theories corresponds as closely with this definition as with any other which can be given.

72

> And when there came a pause
> Of silence such as baffled his best skill:
> Then sometimes, in that silence, while he hung
> Listening, a gentle shock of mild surprise
> Has carried far into his heart the voice
> Of mountain torrents; or the visible scene
> Would enter unawares into his mind
> With all its solemn imagery, its rocks,
> Its woods, and that uncertain heaven received
> Into the bosom of the steady lake.

73

The experience though fugitive and evanescent in the extreme may yet be analysed by a consideration of the occasions on which we became aware of it in a more gradual manner. Limiting ourselves for the moment to the visual field we are aware of certain shapes and colours. These when more closely studied usually reveal themselves as in three dimensions, or as artists say, in forms. These forms must in some cases, but in others may not, be identified as this or that physical object. Throughout this process impulses are aroused and sustained, which gradually increase in variety and degree of systematization. To these systems in their early stages will correspond the emotions such as joy, horror, melancholy, anger, and mirth; or attitudes, such as love, veneration, sentimentality. Songs like this are written:

> Break, break, break,
>   On thy cold gray stones, O Sea!
> And I would that my tongue could utter
>   The thoughts that arise in me.
>
> O well for the fisherman's boy
>   That he shouts with his sister at play!
> O well for the sailor lad,
>   That he sings in his boat on the bay!
>
> And the stately ships go on
>   To their haven under the hill;
> But O for the touch of a vanished hand,
>   And the sound of a voice that is still!

In the interpretation of works of art at an early stage, if we allow ourselves to take on the appropriate mood, we may, XV, come into contact with the personality of the artist.

What he puts into his work is a selection made from an indefinitely large number of possible elements, and their specific arrangement is also only one of many possible. This selection and arrangement is due to the direction and accentuation of his interest – in other words to the play of impulses which controls his activity at the moment; and it is often such that the same group of impulses are aroused in the spectator. We do not make the artist's selection because that is done for us. This seems to be the only way, unless by telepathy, of coming into contact with other minds than our own. Some rest content with this contact, which is plainly a matter of degree.

So far, however, we need not have experienced Beauty, but it is here that our emotion assumes a more general character, and we find that correspondingly our attitude has become impersonal. The explanation of this change is of the greatest importance. The various impulses before alluded to have become further systematized and intensified. Not all impulses, it is plain, as usually excited, are naturally harmonious, for conflict is possible and common. A complete systematization must take the form of such an adjustment as will preserve free play to every impulse, with entire avoidance of frustration. In any equilibrium of this kind, however momentary (cf. Frontispiece), we are experiencing beauty.

The state of equilibrium is not one of passivity, inertia, overstimulation, or conflict, and most people would be rightly dissatisfied with such terms as Nirvana, Ecstasy Sublimation, or At-oneness with Nature,[1] which might at first sight be thought appropriate. As descriptive of an aesthetic state in which impulses are experienced *together*, the word *Synaesthesis*, however, conveniently covers both equilibrium and harmony. The whole subject of Harmony as distinct from Equilibrium requires as careful a treatment, which is attempted by the same authors elsewhere.[2]

---

1 'La beauté anésthetique de la nature', says Lalo (*Introduction à l'Esthétique*, p. 146), 'c'est une sympathie universelle pour la vie et l'être quels qu'ils soient, c'est une intuition panthéistique de la solidarité foncière de toutes choses, ou si l'on veut, c'est le sentiment de la nature: de toute la nature, sans choix aucun, du moins en principe; et non de la 'belle nature'" (Plate A).

2 *Colour-Harmony* (Kegan Paul 1922). It is, perhaps, worthwhile to note that the frequent use of the word Harmony to characterize various mental states felt to be valuable, both by those who aspire to be 'in tune with the Infinite', and by writers on art generally, does not necessarily imply anything in common with that intended here. For example: 'Man is supremely conscious of a dualism within himself – of a war in his members which a higher spiritual harmony alone can quell' (*Hermaia: A Study in Comparative Esthetics*, by Colin McAlpin. p. 363). The dualism is essentially that of Kant or Schiller, if not of Plato's steeds; and similarly when, in the course of her remarks on Empathy, Vernon Lee quotes Fraülein von Ritóok, 'Harmony is the empathic unity of the psychical experience', and adds, 'the microcosm asserts itself with its insistence on plan, unity, harmony... Art would, therefore, be a school for this unity of mood, purpose, and plan, without which consciousness would disintegrate and human life disappear... The unethical, the unintellectual man, like the unaesthetic is the one who is in conflict with himself', the relation to what has been said above

77 In equilibrium, there is no tendency to action, and any concert-goer must have realized the impropriety of the view that action is the proper outcome of aesthetic appreciation. When impulses are 'harmonized' on the other hand they work together, and such disciplined co-ordination in action is much to be desired in other places. When works of art produce such action, or conditions which lead to action they have either not completely fulfilled their function or would in the view of equilibrium here being considered be called not 'beautiful' but 'stimulative'.[1]

78 As we realize beauty we become more fully ourselves the more our impulses are engaged. If, as is sometimes alleged, we are the whole complex of our impulses, this fact would explain itself. Our interest is not canalized in one direction rather than another. It becomes ready instead to take any direction we choose. This is the explanation of that detachment so often

---

may be chiefly verbal. At first sight more hesitation might be felt with the obiter dicta of the eclectic Paul Gaultier who, in his Meaning of Art (trans. 1913) speaks, p. 25, of 'the harmonious and integral expansion of all our nature in the function of feeling', and describes ugliness (p. 59) as 'a rupture of equilibrium, the disorganization of a whole, the result of a conflict of active finalities, which in spite of their opposition are, nevertheless, each for itself elements of harmony'. When, however, Gaultier asks (p. 29), 'Is not aesthetic emotion fundamentally creative of harmony?' and speaks (p. 136) of this emotion making us 'unite our voice in the melody and our active movements with music or the dance', we can answer that as we have endeavoured to show, harmony in this sense is a very different thing from equilibrium.

1 Although the experience here described is readily recognizable this account is admittedly speculative. The argumentative will need no prompting to the remark that the distinction between a balance and a deadlock is difficult to explain. Two particular cases which may produce misapprehension are worth noting.

The first is the case of irresolution. It may be supposed that here we have a balance of impulses by which we seem to be impelled first one way and then another with too rapid an alternation or too weak a thrust for either impulse to take effect. This condition must be marked off as totally distinct from that which we describe as equilibrium. The difference between them is theoretically as follows. In an equilibrium the impulses active, however they are specifically related, do yet sustain one state of mind. They combine to produce one phase of consciousness. In irresolution the sets of impulses sustain severally their independent phases. In some cases what is essentially an oscillation may become a balance. The difference may be found in the cross-connections between the

mentioned in artistic experience.[1] We become impersonal or disinterested.

> Yet once more, O ye Laurels, and once more
> Ye Myrtles brown, with Ivy never-sear,
> I Come to pluck your Berries harsh and crude,
> And with forc'd fingers rude,
> Shatter your leaves before the mellowing year.

Simultaneously, as another aspect of the same adjustment, our individuality becomes differentiated or isolated from the individualities of things around us. We become less 'mixed into'

---

subsidiary impulses contained in these oscillating systems. Two perfectly simple impulses, we may suppose, must either oscillate or lock. A more complex initial conflict may on the other hand discharge itself through its branch connections. We might describe balance as a conflict of impulses solving itself in the arousal of the other impulses of the personality. Balance as we have said above tends to bring the whole of the personality into play.

The other confusing case is that in which no conflict arises because only one self-sufficing set of impulses is in action. The state of mind which then arises seems in many ways to resemble balance. In intense anger or joy for instance we have a certain lucidity, self-possession, and freedom which might be mistaken for some of the conditions which arise in balance. But the resemblances are illusory as time shows. Balance refreshes and never exhausts.

1 In this context the view of those modern psychologists who, like Münsterberg, regard Beauty as an experience of unity projected ('So far as this will is projected into the drama itself, its unity gives us the aesthetic value of a work of art' – 'Music forms an inner world to a unified tissue of volitions', *The Eternal Values*, pp. 200, 252), and occasionally treat this 'unity' as equivalent to 'harmony' (ibid., p. 202), may be contrasted with the following account of Cézanne's attitude:

> L'art est une harmonie parallèle à la nature. Que penser des imbéciles qui vous disent: le peintre est toujours inférieur à la nature! Il lui est parallèle. S'il n'intervient pas volontairement... entendez moi bien. Toute sa volonté doit être de silence. Il doit faire taire en lui toutes les voix préjugés, oublier, oublier, faire silence, être un écho parfait. Alors sur sa plaque sensible, tout le paysage s'inscrira. Pour le fixer sur la toile, l'extérioriser, le métier interviendra ensuite, mais le métier respectueux qui, lui aussi, n'est prêt qu' à obéir, à traduire inconsciemment, tant il sait bien sa langue, le texte qu'il déchiffre, les deux textes parallèles, la nature vive, la nature senti, celle qui est là... (*il montrait la plaine verte et bleue*) celle qui est ici (*il se frappait le front*) qui toutes deux doivent s'amalgamer pour durer.' – Joachim Gasquet, *Cézanne*, p. 81.

other things. As we become more ourselves they become more themselves, because we are less dependent upon the particular impulses which they each arouse in us.

As a corollary of this individualization particular sets of impulses are felt in relation to other sets, which, unless both were already active in the equilibrium, would not occur.[1]

80   EDUCATION

The educative value of art derives partly from this heightened power of differentiation and partly also from the sympathetic understanding of other personalities discussed under the heading of contact above. Art is a means of establishing relations with personalities not otherwise accessible. The gulf which separates us from ancient peoples, savages, enemies, allies, people of another sex, children, or the aged is thus bridged (Plate N). The exertions of the majority of anthropologists might have been more valuable had they not shown themselves unable or unwilling to use this obvious method of understanding.

---

[1] The following quotation may serve as an illustration:

'Well, and what then? You have known a *There* and a *Someone*. The *There* is the future life, the *Someone* is God.'

Prince André did not reply. The carriage and horses had long been led out on to the further bank, and were already harnessed; the sun was half-sunken beneath the horizon, and the evening frost was beginning to encrust the little pools by the shore with starry crystals, while Pierre and André, to the astonishment of the servants, coachmen, and ferryman, still stood in the boat talking.

'If God and the future life exist, then truth and virtue exist; and man's highest happiness consists in striving for their attainment. One must live', said Pierre, 'one must love one must believe that we live, not merely now on this patch of earth, but that we have lived and shall live eternally there in the universe.' He pointed to the sky.

Prince André stood leaning on the rail of the ferry-boat, and listening to Pierre. He never moved his eyes, but gazed at the red reflection of the sun in the dark-blue flood. Pierre ceased speaking. All was silent. The ferry-boat lay drifted along the bank, and only the ripples of the current could be heard lapping feebly against its sides. Prince André fancied that this patter of the water babbled a refrain to Pierre's words, 'That is sooth, accept it: that is sooth, accept it.'

Plate N

Un Papillon (parle).
Mes ailes sont douces comme de la poussière de velours. Je suis tout étonné de vivre. Je ne comprends pas grand'chose, mais je suis beau.
Le pluie facilement dechirerait mon aile rouge et noire qui bat lourdement sur mes pattes.

Such differences as do occur in the experience we feel as an intensification, a broadening, or a deepening of the mood, and may be probably due to the range of impulses involved and their movement about a centre. We experience it under widely different circumstances and in connection with widely different objects not usually considered under categories of art; for instance in the performance of a scientific operation, in the regulation of conduct, or indeed in connection with any natural or imagined object. Descriptions by the poets are abundant.

Early Speculations

Early speculations on the subject of aesthetics were too preoccupied with religious and metaphysical issues to allow any clear statement in this field. Intellectualist theories occasionally allude to harmonious activity. Thus Kant[1] speaks of 'a reciprocal subjective common accord of the power of cognition... The quickening of both faculties (imagination and understanding) to an indefinite but yet, thanks to the given representation, harmonious activity is the sensation whose universal communicability is postulated by the judgment of taste.' And it was Kant's view of the relations of Art and Play which led Schiller in his *Briefe über die ästhetische Erziehung des Menschen* to elaborate a theory of harmonious activity in which a balance or equipoise is maintained.

There are, according to Schiller (Letter 2), two opposing demands in man – that of the sense-impulse, and that of the form-impulse. Whenever the form-impulse prevails (Letter 12) 'there is the highest amplitude of being'. But if we subordinate

---

1 *Critique of Aesthetic Judgement*, trans. Meredith, pp. 59–60.

(Letter 13) the sensuous to the rational, we get mere antagonism and no harmony. Harmony can be attained without diminution of either. And here the function of Play is introduced.

The object of the sense-impulse is *life*, the object of the form-impulse *shape* (Letter 15). The object of the play-impulse, expressed in a general proposition, can then be called *living shape*, or in its widest signification, Beauty. Beauty, then (Letter 16), results from the reciprocity of two opposite impulses, and from the union of the opposite principles: we must seek its highest ideal in the most perfect possible *equipoise*.

'The scales of a balance stand poised', he proceeds (Letter 20), 'when they are empty; but also when they contain equal weights. Thus the mind passes from perception to reflection by an intermediate state (*Stimmung*) in which sense and reason are active at the same time, but thus mutually destroy their determining power and effect a negation through an opposition... if we call the condition of sensuous determination the physical, and that of reflective determination the logical and moral condition, we must call the condition of real and active determinableness the aesthetic condition.' And again, when a thing relates 'to the entirety of our different powers, without being a definite object to any single one of them – that is its *aesthetic* character'.

It will be evident that, as in the case of Kant, the formulation of an aesthetic theory in terms of sense and reason, life and shape, cannot be satisfactory. The ambiguity of such terms makes it doubtful whether Schiller is not describing an ordinary balanced mind of the Aristotelian type. It is easy to describe in haste the experience of Beauty in a way which makes it closely resemble either mystical states or a mere level-headed alertness, or some form of self-contained and controlled sensibility.

> What rigorous calm! What almost holy silence! All the doors are shut, and the beds of flowers are giving out scent; discreetly, of course...
> Two women that lean against each other, stand to the balustrade of red marble on the edge of the terrace.

One of them wishes to speak, to confide to her friend the secret sorrow that is agonizing her heart.

She throws an anxious glance at the motionless leaves, and because of a paroquet with iridescent wings that perches on a branch, she sighs and is silent.

84 If too simple a view of balance be taken, the theory we are describing approximates to a recipe. It is not possible that Goethe may have acted on some such recipe in the construction of *Faust* and *Wilhelm Meister*? In any case the conception of a dual opposition is over-simple, and as Schiller's account which follows would suggest, fails to provide any adequate explanation of the experience he himself describes. The experience of Beauty, he continues (Letter 21), gives us no particular sort of knowledge and has no direct utility, but renders it possible for a man 'to make out of himself what he will, and restores to him the freedom to be what he ought to be'. At the moment, when we are enjoying Beauty (Letter 22) we are 'equally master of our passive and active powers, and with equal facility do we address ourselves to the serious and to sport, to calm and to emotion, to compliance and to resistance, to abstract reflection and to intuition. It is in this state of equanimity and freedom of spirit, united with power and activity, that a genuine work of art should leave us. If, after an enjoyment of this kind we find ourselves predisposed to some one particular mode of feeling or action, unfit for and averse to another', we have, according to Schiller, a certain proof that a purely aesthetic state has not been reached. The following passage from *Resurrection* raises this problem:

85 But here her cry was suddenly changed to moaning, and then died down entirely. One of the attendants caught hold of her arms, which he bound, and the other gagged her with a piece of cloth, which he tied behind her head, so that she might not be able to tear it off.

She looked at the attendants and at the officer with eyes bulging out of their orbits, her whole face jerked, a noisy breath issued from her nose, and her shoulders rose up to her ears and fell again.

'You must not make such a scandal, – I told you so before. It is your own fault', said the officer, going out.

The chimes played in a soft tone, 'How glorious is our Lord in Zion'. The sentries were changed. In the cathedral candles burned, and a sentry stood at the tombs of the Tsars.

Schiller held that no work of art is in reality purely aesthetic, believing that we are not completely prepared for 'abstract reflection directly after lofty musical enjoyment'; though the more universal the medium and the art, the nearer its approximation to the ideal. And, as regards subject, 'true aesthetic freedom is to be expected only from form... and the more imposing and attractive the subject is in itself, or the more inclined the observer is to merge himself immediately in the subject, the more triumphant is the art which overcomes the former and maintains authority over the latter'.

Modern Psychology

It is surprising that, whatever its value, Schiller's theory has not attracted more attention. In Germany it seems to have been absorbed into metaphysical speculations such as those of Schelling, but of recent years it finds a place in the writings of Waldemar Conrad (*Zeitschrift für Ästhetik*, 1912), who related it to the educational ideals of Herbart. Modern psychologists have, in fact, been curiously remiss in this respect with the notable exception of Miss Ethel D. Puffer, who, apparently overlooking Schiller's view, advances a somewhat similar account. At page 50 of her *Psychology of Beauty* we read:

> The psychological organism is in a state of unity either when it is in a state of virtual congealment or emptiness, as in a trance or ecstasy; or when it is in a state of repose, without tendency to change... The only aesthetic repose is that in which stimulation resulting in impulse or movement is checked by its antagonistic impulse, combined with heightening of tone. But this is *tension, equilibrium*, or *balance of forces*, which is thus seen to be a general condition of all aesthetic experience.

The reference to '*its* antagonistic impulse', and 'a general *condition*' are unconvincing; and when Miss Puffer goes on to say that 'the concept is familiar in pictorial composition', and adds (p. 125) that it is not beauty we seek from Hogarth and Goya, it is clear that she expects always to find the cause of balance in the construction of the work of art. Thus she quotes in favour of her view of Goya the following striking extract from Klinger on the subject of 'background': 'Such a tone is the foil for psychological moments, as they are handled by Goya, for instance, with barbarically magnificent nakedness. On a background which is merely indicated, with few strokes which hardly indicate space, he impales like a butterfly the human type, mostly in a moment of folly or wickedness', which does as much as any description can to show the kind of beauty Goya realized – a beauty obviously not of the objective (formal) kind which is all she is able to admit in satirical work. All through her treatment this assumption of an objective balance is in evidence, culminating in the final chapter, where (p. 279) a relapse into emotional expressionism occurs, in an attempt to discover such objective balance in moral ideas. The essential criticism of such an attempt is that an objective balance, as we have already stated, may indeed predispose to, but is not necessarily followed by, equilibrium; and, further, this objective balance must be capable of being independently ascertained, not merely inferred from a subjective state.[1]

> I there before thee, in the country that well thou knowest,
> Already arrived am inhaling the odorous air:
> I watch thee enter unerringly where thou goest,
> And anchor queen of the strange shipping there,

---

[1] It is a pity that so interesting a study should have so chaotic a conclusion. What, for example, is to be understood by the following remarks?:

> That part of the effect of beauty in a picture which is due to the idea is thus the fundamental but merely abstract element of unity, contributing to the complex aesthetic state only the simplest condition (p. 279)... Such specific emotion as may be detected in any aesthetic experience is, then, covered by the definition of beauty only in so far as it has become form rather than content – is valuable only in its relations rather than in itself (p. 283).

Thy sails for awnings spread, thy masts bare;
Nor is ought from the foaming reef to the snow-capp'd,
    grandest
Peak, that is over the feathery palms more fair
Than thou, so upright, so stately, and still thou standest.[1]

A more solid and satisfactory adaptation of this theory of equilibrium to the modern psychology of appreciation may be found in W. M. Urban's *Valuation* (p. 219), where it appears as

> the concept of the widened ground of diffused stimulation, the *balance* of impulses, so that no one shall constitute an illusion-disturbing moment and lead to readjustment in a new value movement; the consequent *repose* of conation[2] in the object and the *expansion* of feeling which goes with it. The ordering, rearrangement of content characteristic of the aesthetic experience is, therefore, in the service of the deepening, or enhancement of that fundamental mode of worth experience which is appreciatively described as the immanental reference [...][3]

---

1 Contrast the following by the same writer for formal balance *without* synaesthesis:

Thou, careless, awake!
  Thou peacemaker, fight!
Stand England for honour
  And God guard the Right!
etc.

2 Editorial Note: Both the original journal publication, 'The Sense of Beauty' (1921) and all original publications read 'repose of emotion in the object', which though an understandable error is potentially very confusing.

3 This enhancement must not be confused with intensity or height of vitality. It is often suggested that, XIV, heightening vitality, which is usually an important accompaniment of the appreciation of good work (cf. Plate O), is the chief aim of art. It may be readily admitted that mental and physical fitness is closely allied to equilibrium, but although equilibrium certainly conduces to health (promotes, e.g., the circulation of the blood and raises the general tone of the body), and health facilitates equilibrium, yet this is no reason for confusing the functions of the Studio and the Gymnasium.

Editorial Note: Wilbur Marshall Urban, *Valuation: Its Nature and Laws* (Swan Sonnenschein: London, 1909), 219.

Plate O

And, again, in primitive dances the object of desire, whether martial, erotic, or religious is 'distanced',[1] and 'the fundamental conation becomes dispositional. This rhythm, usually of the form of advance or retreat, of affirmation and arrest of expression, produces an equilibrium of impulses, which prevents the fundamental tendency from breaking forth into overt action.'[2]

It might be assumed from these quotations that Urban's account is identical with that which we have given above, but this is by no means the case, for his masterly systematization has the defects of its qualities. In the process of erecting his monumental edifice he has sometimes been led to build with material of imperfect homogeneity, and has consequently incorporated in the fabric elements which are essentially disruptive. Combined with his analysis of the equilibration of impulses are importations from the systems of Marshall[3] and Groos, which falsify the description of the way in which equilibrium is brought about. In particular, the constant reference to 'illusion-disturbing moments' in accordance with the theory of Groos that the elimination of these disturbing moments is necessary to the 'Aesthetic illusion', vitiates the account of the balance which it is supposed to explain.

CONCLUSION

In conclusion, the reason why equilibrium is a justification for the preference of one experience before another, is the fact that it brings into play all our faculties. In virtue of what we have called the synaesthetic character of the experience, we are ena-

---

1 A development of this view of distance will be found in Mr E. Bullough's article on 'Psychical distance' in the *British Journal of Psychology* (1912–13, p. 87). Such 'distancing' would, however, on any interpretation seem to be far from essential in the description of aesthetic experience.

2 Editorial Note: *Valuation*, p. 226.

3 Marshall, both in his *Aesthetic Principles*, p. 186, and *Pain, Pleasure, and Aesthetics*, p. 332, is led by his hedonic assumptions to construct elaborate hypotheses as to the way in which the artist succeeds in 'widening' and giving permanence to the pleasures he is supposed to be concerned with. Such constructions cannot be profitably incorporated in an account so differently orientated as the above.

bled, as we have seen (p. 79) to appreciate relationships in a way which would not be possible under normal circumstances. Through no other experience can the full richness and complexity of our environment be realized. The ultimate value of equilibrium is that it is better to be fully than partially alive.

93 When we have intelligence resulting from sincerity this condition is to be ascribed to nature; when we have sincerity resulting from intelligence, this condition is to be ascribed to instruction. But given the sincerity and there shall be the intelligence; given the intelligence and there shall be the sincerity.

To this attainment there are requisite the extensive study of what is excellent, accurate enquiry about it, careful reflection on it, the clear discrimination of it, and the earnest practise of it.

Let a man proceed in this way and though dull he will surely become intelligent; though weak, he will surely become strong.

From The Chung Yung: The Doctrine of Equilibrium and Harmony

INDEX
AUTHORS AND ARTISTS REFERRED TO

Editorial Note: The index numbers refer to the pages of the original edition, which are found in the margin of the current text. The original index represents page numbers referring to the principal discussion of an author in bold type of a larger point size; here they are represented in italics.

Alexander 48
Allen 48, *50–51*
Aristotle 26, 35
Arnold 37

Baudelaire 42
Bell 15, 27, 31, 51, *57–59*
Berenson 67
Bergson 34
Bosanquet 15, *46*, 48
Bullough 89

Carpenter 49
Carritt 45
Cézanne 78
Chang 13
Clutton-Brock 41
Coleridge 37, 61
Confucius 72
Conrad 86
Croce 15, 36, *43–46*

Delacroix 31

Eastlake 36, 35
Eddington 45
Eliot 47

Fouillée 48
Fry 23, *60–61*

Gasquet 78
Gaultier 76
Goethe 84
Goya 87
Groos 70, 90
Guyau 47

Haydon 49

Hearn 32
Herbart 86
Hogarth 51, 87

Johnson 51

Kant 33, 76, 81, 83
Kirschman 23
Klinger 87
Knight 61
Külpe 33

Laird 23, 48
Lalo 26, 75
Lange 39
Lee 51, *68,* 70, 76
Lethaby 40
Lipps *65–67*, 70
Lotze 65

McAlpin 76
McDowall 45, 49
Marriott 29
Marshall 90
Millet 42, 55
Morris 40
Münsterberg 67, 78
Murry 41

Plato 76
Puffer *86–87*

Rembrandt 55
Rolland 40
Ross 48
Ruge 34
Ruskin 15, *40*
Rymer 36

Santayana 15, 52
Schelling 86
Schiller 76, *81–86*
Schopenhauer 33
Shakespeare 36
Souriau 66
Spencer *49–50*
Strauss 55

Tchaikovsky 55
Tolstoy 15, 40, 61

Urban 89–90

Von Ritóok 76

PASSAGES QUOTED

Keats, 'Ode on a Grecian Urn', 9.

Eastlake, *The Fine Arts*, 10.

Shakespeare, *Coriolanus*, 10.

Coleridge, 'The Aeolian Harp', 10.

Psalm CXXXVII, Trans. Coverdale, 11.

Shelley. 'Ariel to Miranda', 19.

Hooker, *Ecclesiastical Polity (Preface)*, 24.

Shelley, *Queen Mab*, 25.

Burns, 'Auld Lang Syne', 26.

Burns 'I hae a wife', 28.

Shakespeare, *Cymbeline*, 31.

Byron, *Childe Harold*, Canto 4, 32.

Byron, *Childe Harold* Canto 4, 36.

Wordsworth, 'Sonnet composed upon the beach near Calais', 45.

Scot, 'Coronach', 47.

Whitman 'Lo Victress on the Peaks', 53.

Shakespeare, *Henry IV, Part II*, 55.

Shelley, 'The Triumph of Life', 57.

Keats, 'I stood tip-toe upon a little hill', 57.

Swinburne, 'Tiresias', 59.

Wordsworth, *Prelude*, 62.

Tennyson, 'Break, break, break', 63.

Milton, *Lycidas*, 66.

Tolstoy, *War and Peace*, 67.

Jammes, *Existences*, 69.

Thou-sin-yu, *Trans. Mathers*, 70.

Bridges, 'A passer by', 73.

EDITORIAL APPENDIX
PREFACE TO THE FIRST EDITION OF 1922

Interest in questions of Aesthetics has been greatly stimulated during the past few years both by a wider knowledge of non-European – particularly of Eastern and primitive – Art, and by the rapid development of Psychology as a science. Traditional methods of approach equally with vague philosophical speculations have been found inadequate, and the need for a new orientation is evident to most students of recent theoretical publications.

In the following pages an attempt is made to present in a condensed form the greater part of accredited opinion on the subject, and to relate the views thus presented to the main positions from which the theory of art-criticism may proceed. It is hoped that in this way it will serve either as an introduction to those who from a literary point of view or as practical artists are interested in the problems which divergences of aesthetic judgements raise, or as a textbook for students of the Theory of Criticism itself. The discussion therefore follows a rather unusual course, its aim being not to bring theories into opposition with one another, but by distinguishing them to allow to each its separate sphere of validity. If verbal conflicts are avoided, there will be seen to be many possible theories of Beauty, not one only, the understanding of which may help in the appreciation of Art.

The attitude of tolerance which this treatment implies may require a corresponding effort on the part of the reader. Much that on first inspection appears inconclusive or obscure, will it is hoped, be better understood as the partial separation of the fields dealt with by the different theories is more clearly realized. The theory of Synaesthesis with which our discussion ends is, however, in a special position. The term Synaesthesis itself is selected to cover the two experiences suggested by Confucius in the

PREFACE TO THE FIRST EDITION OF 1922

passage which appears at the beginning of our enquiry; and it is thought that the account of Equilibrium is of sufficient importance, not only as an explanation of the aesthetic experiences described by many of the greatest and most sensitive artists and critics of the past, but also in psychological theory, to justify a claim that it should be regarded as the theory of Beauty *par excellence*. Such an ethical judgement, which is, however, independent of our main exposition, implies the suggestion that if the word 'Beauty' is to be used consistently in some one field, the definition in terms of Equilibrium is most worthy of consideration.

7   The appreciation of Beauty, whether in Painting, Music or Poetry or in everyday experience, cannot but be developed by a clearer knowledge of what it is and where it may be looked for, and an acquaintance with the opinions of artists and philosophers on this subject will assist those who wish to increase their powers of discrimination and thereby to lay the foundations of a genuine and at the same time personal taste. It should also be noted that by uniting varied qualifications the authors have been enabled to treat the subject in a more catholic fashion than is usual, and to make it less likely that any important aspect of interest to the general reader has been overlooked.

It remains to add a brief reference to the quotations and the reproductions. When no other object is expressly stated, quotations provide a concrete illustration of some critical point discussed in the passage immediately preceding, and are therefore not to be regarded as additional commentary. They are intended mainly as a constant reminder of what the discussion is about, and are given as fully as space permits in order that the reader may have this opportunity of escaping from the scientific language of the argument. And as regards the reproductions, most of which have been specially made for the purpose, it is hardly necessary to add that they are not put forward as the 'Best pictures', nor are they typical in all cases of their period or place of

8   origin. Each, however, adequately illustrates one *or more* of the theories discussed, and it will be obvious that all of them are

works of high rank. For permission to photograph the Hogarth (Plate H) we have to thank the Directors of the Foundling Hospital. Plates B, C, and O are the copyright of the Folkwang Verlag, Hagen, i.W., Plate D of Messrs. Braun & Co., and Plate G of the International Portrait Service. The Chinese painting on silk (Plate N) is darkened with age and this has made its adequate reproduction a matter of considerable difficulty. In the Frontispiece and Plates G, I, and N, details only are given, as the presentation of the entire picture on so small a scale would have rendered appreciation impossible. We are indebted to Mr. C. H. Hsu for writing the Chinese characters which signify the Doctrine of Equilibrium and Harmony.

C. K. O.
I. A. R.
J. W.